THE AMERICAN CIVIL WAR

BY RICH

CW00872179

Published by

Contents

Introduction

In recognition of the 150th anniversary of the Battle of Gettysburg, we have decided to put together a source that will provide a collection of information on various aspects of this conflict and the entire War Between the States.

This book provides detailed information on famous generals, women, battles, weapons, music and horses, Civil War reenacting, haunted Civil War sites and battlefield preservation. It was a massive undertaking, and still only scratches the surface of this fascinating subject.

The amount of information on the American Civil War is incredible, so we attempted to provide information that will make different aspects of the conflict understandable. We hope this will prove a valuable asset to anyone who is interested in this topic. This should prove especially useful to students doing research on these topics. What school-age child is not fascinated by this subject?

After completely reading this book, students should be able to discuss some of the social and political issues that people confronted during the Civil War, use the Internet to locate additional sources for further enrichment and discuss the issues and their reactions to those issues from multiple perspectives.

While working on a project about the American Civil War, we discovered that an alarming number of Civil War Battlefields are in danger of being lost forever. This prompted us to join the Civil War Preservation Trust in soliciting help to save our nation's heritage.

Please join us on our journey from the first shot fired at Fort Sumter to the surrender at Appomattox Court House. Along the way, you will learn about some famous events and the people involved. You will also learn about some of the reason the war happened, some of its consequences and maybe even have some fun.

The battle has begun...

What is a Civil War?

A Civil War is a war in which factions from the same nation, area, culture or society fight for control of an area or for political power. It is a violent struggle for power. During the American Civil War, one part of the nation tried to break away, while the other tried to prevent its succession, causing armies from both sides to clash.

A Civil War can be considered a revolution if major restructuring of the society takes place, such as during the American Revolution. Revolutions are usually fought over issues of ideology. The first example of a revolution was the French Revolution, which pitted the poor people of France against the monarchy.

Civil Wars can be fought over religion, such as during Germany's Thirty Years' War and in the conflicts in Northern Ireland. Competition for resources or economic gain is a frequent cause of Civil Wars.

Putting a society back together after a Civil War can be difficult, since both parties will still be occupying the same areas. Both factions must learn to coexist with each other once again. There can be hard feelings for many generations.

What Caused the Civil War?

The American Civil War was fought between two dozen Northern states and the eleven Southern states that seceded from the Union in 1861. Before the war was over there were almost a million casualties (3% of the population), and approximately 561,000 deaths. More American lives were lost than in any other conflict in U. S. history.

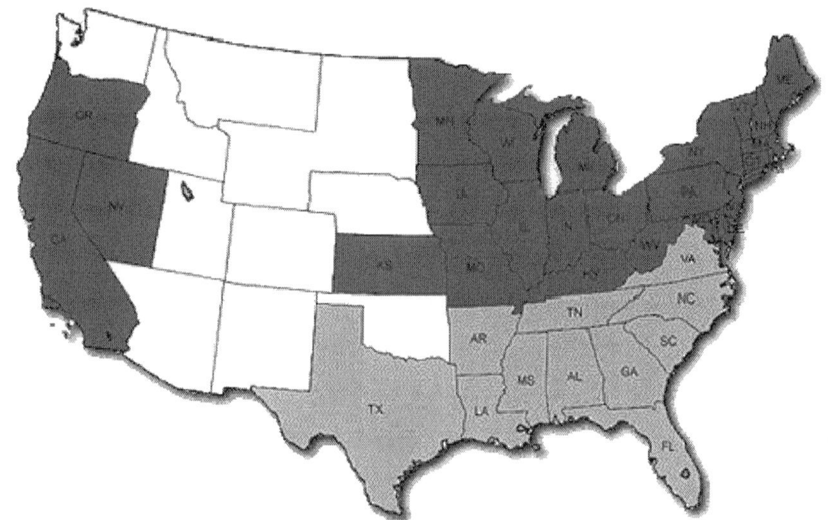

The Union states included: California, Connecticut, Delaware, Illinois, Indiana, Iowa, Kansas, Kentucky, Maine, Maryland, Massachusetts, Michigan, Minnesota, Missouri, New Hampshire, New Jersey, New York, Ohio, Oregon, Pennsylvania, Rhode Island, Vermont, and Wisconsin.

Colorado, Dakota, Nebraska, Nevada, New Mexico, Utah, and Washington also fought on the Union side as territories as they were not yet states.

South Carolina, Mississippi, Florida, Alabama, Georgia, Louisiana and Texas seceded shortly after the election of Abraham Lincoln.

The Southern states, where slavery and cotton plantation agriculture were common, formed the Confederate States of America in 1861, with Jefferson Davis as President, and a constitution modeled after that of the North.

The Confederates attacked Fort Sumter in 1861 and President Lincoln called for troops to reclaim U. S. territory, resulting in the secession of four more states, including Virginia, Arkansas, North Carolina and Tennessee.

The northwestern counties of Virginia re-entered the Union in 1863 as West Virginia. Four more slave states including: Maryland, Delaware, Missouri, and Kentucky did not secede, and became known as the Border States.

Both Missouri and Kentucky remained in the Union, but factions within each state organized desired secession.

The Civil War began when the South opened fire on Fort Sumter in South Carolina on April 12, 1861. The first shot of the war was fired by Private Edmund Ruffin. Although the bombardment lasted more than 39 hours, there were no deaths on either side.

At the beginning of the conflict, Northern soldiers were only signed up for ninety days, which was the length of time they thought it would take to force the Southern forces to surrender. They were in for a big surprise when the Confederacy put up a fight. It is estimated that almost 11,000 military incidents took place ranging from major battles to minor skirmishes.

Many of the early battles of the war were won by the South and Lincoln was forced to replace his commanding officers several times. The commander of the Army of Northern Virginia, General Robert E. Lee, waged a fierce battle and even invaded Northern territory, getting as far north as Gettysburg, Pennsylvania in July of 1863, where he was forced to retreat. After that loss, the Confederate forces suffered many more defeats at the hands of the Union.

General Ulysses S. Grant was made commander of all Union forces in 1864 and decided to wage a total war against the Confederates, destroying some areas completely. He surrounded General Lee's troops at Appomattox Courthouse on April 9, 1865, and they were forced to surrender. However, news was slow to travel and the last Southern troops did not surrender until November, 1865.

During the war, U.S. forces were commonly referred to as "the Union,", "Federals", "the North," or "Yankees," while the Confederates were usually called "the Confederacy," "the South," or "Rebels." Soldiers who fought for the Union were referred to as "Billy Yanks;" those who fought for the Confederacy were called "Johnny Rebs."

After the war, the country went through a period of Reconstruction where the Confederate states were slowly reintegrated into the Union. The period is marred by corruption and a lack of rights which lasted until 1878.

Questions remain today as to the legality of Lincoln's actions. Did the Southern states have the right to secede? The Constitution does not state the Union is permanent and in fact many states ratified it only under the condition that they could secede at any time.

It should be noted that no Confederate leader was ever brought to trial fro treason, because that would have caused a verdict to be rendered on the constitutionality of secession.

Another important question to consider is: If the South had succeeded, could the two nations have existed separately? Possibly not, as the South controlled the crops and the North controlled the industry. It took both halves of the country to make it a great and powerful nation.

What's In A Name?

The American Civil War has been known by numerous names that reflect the historical, political, and cultural sensitivities of different groups and regions. Unlike other civil wars, the conflict was not fought over control of a government, but was fought over a secession attempt.

The most common term for the conflict is the "Civil War." Abraham Lincoln used it in his Gettysburg Address (.".. Now we are engaged in a great civil war. ...).

"The War Between the States" has been used widely in the South. It was rarely used during the war itself, but first became popular in 1868 when former Confederate Vice President Alexander Stephens published his book, *A Constitutional View of the Late War Between the States.*

In the 1880s, the term "War of the Rebellion" achieved some prominence in the North, but it was considered a negative term by Southerners. Although Confederates during the war frequently used the term "Rebels" to describe themselves, this was considered to be derogatory when spoken by a Northerner.

"War between the United States of America and the Confederate States of America" was the official term used in documents in Richmond during the war.

"War of Southern Independence" was popular on the Confederate side during the war itself, although the term's popularity fell in the aftermath of the Confederacy's failure to gain independence.

"War of Northern Aggression" was the term used by Confederates to suggest that the North invaded the South.

"War for States' Rights" was not used by historians before 1990. It is a modern term used by "neo-Confederates" to promote a political agenda.

Other names that were popular in the South were "War in Defense of Virginia," "Mr. Lincoln's War," and "War of Secession." Names popular in the North included "War of the Insurrection," "War to Save the Union," "War for Abolition" and "War to Prevent Southern Independence."

- **Here are a few more:**
- The War for Constitutional Liberty
- The Second American Revolution
- The Southern Rebellion
- The War for Southern Rights
- The War of the Southern Planters
- The Second War of Independence
- The War to Suppress Yankee Arrogance
- The Brother's War
- The War of Secession
- The Great Rebellion
- The War for Nationality
- The War for Southern Nationality
- The War Against Slavery
- The Civil War Between the States
- The War of the Sixties
- The Yankee Invasion
- The War for Separation
- The War for Abolition

- The War for the Union
- The Confederate War
- The War of the Southrons
- The War for Southern Freedom
- The War of the North and the South
- The War
- The Late Unpleasantness
- The Lost Cause
- The Late Friction
- The Late Ruction
- The Schism
- The Uncivil War

The Cost in Lives

Quite often, people forget that soldiers are people who have lives. When one speaks about casualties, they are talking about injury or loss of life. The Civil War cost more Americans their lives than all other wars in the history of this country. Some of the battles stand out as especially horrific. It is amazing to think that more men died during the three days at Gettysburg, than during the almost four years in Korea.

Ten Bloodiest Battles of the Civil War

Gettysburg	40,638
Chickamauga	28,399
Seven Days	27,535
Antietam	23,381
Wilderness	22,033
Chancellorsville	21,862
Atlanta	19,715
Second Manassas	19,204
Stones River	18,459
Shiloh	17,897

American Deaths in All Wars

Revolutionary War (1775-1783)	4,435
War of 1812 (1812-1815)	2,260
Mexican War (1846-1848)	13,283
Civil War (1861-1865)	623,026
Spanish-American War (1898)	2,446
World War I (1917-1918)	116,708
World War II (1941-1945)	407,316
Korean War (1950-1953)	36,914
Vietnam War (1964-1973)	58,169
Persian Gulf War (1991)	269

Slavery and Abolition

Slavery is the practice of keeping people as property against their will and forcing them to serve. Slaves in the United States remained enslaved until the ratification of the Thirteenth Amendment to the Constitution in 1865.

Twenty blacks were brought by a Dutch ship and sold to the colony of Jamestown in 1619. Three are believed to have been named Isabella, Antoney and Pedro. William Tucker, the son of two of these slaves is considered the first African-American born in North America.

Almost all slaves were blacks. In the beginning, slaves were used mostly in the Southern colonies, although there were a few in the Northern colonies also. Slaves were most useful in an agricultural setting. Many landowners began to grow increasingly dependent on slave labor for their livelihood.

Rhode Island was the first state to ban slavery in 1794, but after the invention of the cotton gin, the demand for cotton grew, and so did the need for slave labor on cotton plantations.

The U. S. Constitution, adopted in 1787, prevented Congress from banning the importation of slaves before 1808, so that any new slaves would have to be descendants of ones that were currently in the US.

History shows that many slave owners were cruel, denying their slaves the rights enjoyed by free people. Some owners practiced chopping off the limbs of slaves who tried to run away, while others whipped them frequently.

An area free of slavery was formed north of the Ohio River, however the law stated that escaped slaves in Northern territories be returned to their owners as they were still considered property.

During the first half of the 1800's a movement to end slavery called abolitionism, grew in strength in the North. This took place in contrast to strong support of slavery in the South. Even many of those that were against slavery did not consider the black man to be a real person.

Some well-known leaders of the abolition movement included Harriet Beecher Stowe, John Brown, Frederick Douglass and Harriet Tubman, who helped 350 slaves escape from the South and became known as a conductor on the Underground Railroad.

Refugees from slavery fled the South across the Ohio River to the North via this Underground Railroad. Abolitionists clashed with slave-owners many times throughout the century. The Missouri Compromise of 1820 was an attempt to make sure that the two interests were balanced in the U. S. Senate.

The radical abolitionist John Brown was hanged for his attempt to lead a total slave revolt. Abraham Lincoln, who was opposed to the expansion of slavery, although not to slavery itself, was elected in 1860. He did not appear on the ballots of most southern states as many in the South feared that his real intent was the complete abolition of slavery in every state. Many people feared that the sudden freeing of 4 million slaves would mean trouble. The combination of these factors led the South to secede from the Union beginning the American Civil War.

The Civil War led to the end of slavery in the United States. Lincoln's Emancipation Proclamation of 1863 was a purely symbolic gesture, meant actually to punish the South, that proclaimed freedom for slaves within the Confederacy, although not for those in the important border states of Tennessee, Maryland and Delaware fearing that they would secede as well.

Legally, slaves within the United States remained slaves until the final ratification of the Thirteenth Amendment to the Constitution in 1865, eight months after the end of the war.

One of the most famous slavery incidents concerned Dred Scott, who sued in an attempt to gain his freedom. His case was based on the fact, that he and his wife Harriet had lived in states where slavery was illegal.

Scott was born in 1799 in Virginia as property of the Blow family. Due to financial issues, he was sold to Dr. John Emerson, a doctor in the U.S. Army. Dred met his wife on a trip and she returned to Missouri with him and the Emersons. Dr. Emerson died in 1843 and Mrs. Emerson's brother became executor of the estate, making the Scotts slaves again.

Scott sued in 1847, losing the first time, but winning in 1850. In 1852, the Missouri Supreme Court reversed the decision, making them slaves again. In 1857, the Supreme Court declared that slaves were property and had no claim to freedom. Scott was returned to the Blow family, who granted him his freedom. He died of tuberculosis in 1858.

Battlefields of the Civil War

Fort Sumter

Northern Name for Battle: Ft. Sumter
Southern Name for Battle: Ft. Sumter
Location of Battle: Charleston County, South Carolina
Date of Battle: April 12-14, 1861
Northern Commander: Robert Anderson
Southern Commander: P.G.T. Beauregard
Winner: Confederates
Northern Troops Involved: 85
Southern Troops Involved: 500
Northern Casualties: 3
Southern Casualties: 0
Interesting Facts: This was the first battle of the Civil War. It consisted of a 39 hour shelling of the fort by the Confederates, after which, the Northern troops surrendered. There were no deaths on either side.

First Bull Run

Northern Name for Battle: First Manassas
Southern Name for Battle: First Bull Run
Location of Battle: Fairfax County and Prince William County, Virginia
Date of Battle: July 21, 1861
Northern Commander: Irvin McDowell
Southern Commander: Pierre Gustave Toutant Beauregard
Winner: Confederates
Northern Troops Involved: 28,450
Southern Troops Involved: 32,230
Northern Casualties: 2,645
Southern Casualties: 1,981
Interesting Facts: This was the second battle of the war.

Wilson's Creek

Northern Name for Battle: Wilson's Creek
Southern Name for Battle: Wilson's Creek
Location of Battle: Springfield, Missouri
Date of Battle: August 10, 1861
Northern Commander: Nathaniel Lyon
Southern Commander: Ben McCulloch and Sterling Price
Winner: Confederate
Northern Troops Involved: 5,400
Southern Troops Involved: 11,600
Northern Casualties: 1,236
Southern Casualties: 1,184
Interesting Facts: The Confederates outnumbered the Union by more than two-to-one in this battle.

Fort Henry

Northern Name for Battle: Fort Henry
Southern Name for Battle: Fort Henry
Location of Battle: Stewart County and Henry County, Tennessee and Calloway County, Kentucky
Date of Battle: February 6, 1862
Northern Commanders: Ulysses S. Grant and Andrew H. Foote
Southern Commander: Lloyd Tilghman
Winner: Union
Northern Troops Involved: 17,000
Southern Troops Involved: 3,000
Northern Casualties: 45
Southern Casualties: 79
Interesting Facts: This battle was fought in two different states.

Fort Donelson

Northern Name for Battle: Fort Donelson
Southern Name for Battle: Fort Donelson
Location of Battle: Stewart County, Tennessee
Date of Battle: February 12-16, 1862
Northern Commander: Ulysses S. Grant
Southern Commanders: John B. Hood and Simon B. Buckner
Winner: Union
Northern Troops Involved: 27,000
Southern Troops Involved: 21,000
Northern Casualties: 2,832
Southern Casualties: 16,623
Interesting Facts: Grant earned the nickname "Unconditional Surrender" Grant at this battle.

Pea Ridge

Northern Name for Battle: Pea Ridge
Southern Name for Battle: Pea Ridge
Location of Battle: Benton County, Arkansas
Date of Battle: March 6-8, 1862
Northern Commander: Samuel R. Curtis
Southern Commanders: Earl Van Dorm
Winner: Union
Northern Troops Involved: 11,250
Southern Troops Involved: 14,000
Northern Casualties: 1,384
Southern Casualties: 800
Interesting Facts: The Union had complete control of Missouri after this battle

Hampton Roads

Northern Name for Battle: Hampton Roads
Southern Name for Battle: Hampton Roads
Location of Battle: Hampton Roads, Virginia
Date of Battle: March 8-9, 1862
Northern Commander: John Warden
Southern Commanders: Franklin Buchanan and Catesby R. Jones
Winner: Tie
Northern Troops Involved: 2,512
Southern Troops Involved: 188
Northern Casualties: 409
Southern Casualties: 60
Interesting Facts: This was the first battle fought with ironclads.

Shiloh

Northern Name for Battle: Shiloh
Southern Name for Battle: Battle of Pittsburg Landing
Location of Battle: Harden County, Tennessee
Date of Battle: April 6-7, 1862
Northern Commander: Ulysses S. Grant
Southern Commander: Albert Sydney Johnston
Winner: Union
Northern Troops Involved: 63,000
Southern Troops Involved: 40,000
Northern Casualties: 13,047
Southern Casualties: 10,694
Interesting Facts: This was the bloodiest battle up to that time.

Williamsburg

Northern Name for Battle: Williamsburg
Southern Name for Battle: Williamsburg
Location of Battle: Williamsburg, VA
Date of Battle: May 5, 1862
Northern Commander: McClellan
Southern Commander: Longstreet
Winner: Tie
Northern Troops Involved: 87,000
Southern Troops Involved: 45,000
Northern Casualties: 2,283
Southern Casualties: 1,560
Interesting Facts: This was the first battle of the Peninsula Campaign.

Fair Oaks

Northern Name for Battle: Fair Oaks
Southern Name for Battle: Seven Pines
Location of Battle: Henrico County, Virginia
Date of Battle: May 31-July 1, 1862
Northern Commander: George Brinton McClellan
Southern Commanders: Joseph Eggleston Johnston and Robert E. Lee
Winner: Union
Northern Troops Involved: 42,000
Southern Troops Involved: 42,000
Northern Casualties: 5,031
Southern Casualties: 6,124
Interesting Facts: Because Johnston was wounded in this battle, General Robert E. Lee took full control of the Army of Northern Virginia.

Gaines' Mill

Northern Name for Battle: Gaines' Mill
Southern Name for Battle: Gaines' Mill
Location of Battle: Washington County, Maryland
Date of Battle: June 27, 1862
Northern Commander: F.J. Porter
Southern Commander: Robert E. Lee
Winner: Confederate
Northern Troops Involved: 34,214
Southern Troops Involved: 57018
Northern Casualties: 6,800
Southern Casualties: 1,560
Interesting Facts: Several of McClellan's subordinates urged him to attack John Magruder's division, but he didn't because he believed there was far more confederates than there really was.

Savages Station

Northern Name for Battle: Savages Station
Southern Name for Battle: Savages Station
Location of Battle: Henrico County, VA
Date of Battle: June 29, 1862
Northern Commander: Edwin Sumner
Southern Commander: John Magruder
Winner: tie
Northern Troops Involved: 87,000
Southern Troops Involved: 45,000
Northern Casualties: 1,200
Southern Casualties: 3,500
Interesting Facts: Only two of the seven attacks planned by the confederates actually happened

Glendale

Northern Name for Battle: Glendale
Southern Name for Battle: Glendale
Location of Battle: Glendale, VA
Date of Battle: June 30, 1862
Northern Commander: George B. McClellan
Southern Commander: Robert E. Lee
Winner: Tie
Northern Troops Involved: 13,539
Southern Troops Involved: unknown
Northern Casualties: 2,700
Southern Casualties: 3,600
Interesting Facts: This battle has six different names. Glendale, Frayser's Farm, Nelson's Farm, Charles City Crossroads, New Market Road, or Riddell's Shop.

Malvern Hill

Northern Name for Battle: Malvern Hill
Southern Name for Battle: Malvern Hill
Location of Battle: Malvern Hill, Virginia
Date of Battle: July 1, 1862
Northern Commander: George B. McClellan
Southern Commander: Robert E. Lee
Winner: Union
Northern Troops Involved: unknown
Southern Troops Involved: unknown
Northern Casualties: 3,214
Southern Casualties: 5,355
Interesting Facts: This was the last battle of Seven Days.

Second Bull Run

Northern Name for Battle: Second Manassas
Southern Name for Battle: Second Bull Run
Location of Battle: Prince William County, Virginia
Date of Battle: Aug 29-30, 1862
Northern Commander: John Pope
Southern Commander: Robert E. Lee
Winner: Confederates
Northern Troops Involved: 63,000
Southern Troops Involved: 54,000
Northern Casualties: 14,754
Southern Casualties: 8,397
Interesting Facts: One fourth of the Union troops present died in this battle.

Seven Days

Northern Name for Battle: Battle of Seven Days
Southern Name for Battle: Battle of Seven Days
Location of Battle: Multiple locations in Virginia
Date of Battle: June 25-July 1, 1862
Northern Commander: George B. McClellan
Southern Commander: Robert Edward Lee
Winner: Confederates
Northern Troops Involved: 91,000
Southern Troops Involved: 95,000
Northern Casualties: 15,849
Southern Casualties: 20,141
Interesting Facts: This battle was actually many different battles fought over a week-long period.

Richmond

Northern Name for Battle: Richmond
Southern Name for Battle: Richmond
Location of Battle: Richmond, Kentucky
Date of Battle: August 29-30, 1862
Northern Commander: William Nelson
Southern Commander: Kirby Smith
Winner: Confederates
Northern Troops Involved: unknown
Southern Troops Involved: 6,500
Northern Casualties: 4,900
Southern Casualties: 750
Interesting Facts: This was the most overwhelming confederate victory of the war.

Harper's Ferry

Northern Name for Battle: Harper's Ferry
Southern Name for Battle: Harper's Ferry
Location of Battle: Washington County, Maryland
Date of Battle: September 12-15, 1862
Northern Commander: Dixon Miles
Southern Commander: Stonewall Jackson
Winner: Confederates
Northern Troops Involved: 14,000
Southern Troops Involved: 19,900
Northern Casualties: 12,476
Southern Casualties: 286
Interesting Facts: During the second day of fighting, Col. Ford fell ill, and left the fighting to Col. Eliakim Sherrill. Shortly after he was shot and left all of the fighting to Major Sylvester Hewitt.

Munfordville

Northern Name for Battle: Munfordville
Southern Name for Battle: Munfordville
Location of Battle: Munfordville, KY.
Date of Battle: September 14-17, 1862
Northern Commander: John Wilder
Southern Commander: Braxton Bragg
Winner: Confederate
Northern Troops Involved: 4,000
Southern Troops Involved: unknown
Northern Casualties: 4,148
Southern Casualties: 714
Interesting Facts: This victory allowed the confederates to have a temporary hold on the region, and impair the union supply lines.

Antietam

Northern Name for Battle: Antietam
Southern Name for Battle: Sharpsburg
Location of Battle: Washington County, Maryland
Date of Battle: September 17, 1862
Northern Commander: George B. McClellan
Southern Commander: Ambrose Powell Hill
Winner: Tie
Northern Troops Involved: 87,000
Southern Troops Involved: 45,000
Northern Casualties: 12,410
Southern Casualties: 13,724
Interesting Facts: This battle is considered the bloodiest single day battle of the Civil War.

South Mountain

Northern Name for Battle: South Mountain
Southern Name for Battle: South Mountain
Location of Battle: Frederick County and Washington County, Maryland
Date of Battle: September 14, 1862
Northern Commander: George B. McClellan
Southern Commander: Robert E. Lee
Winner: Union
Northern Troops Involved: 28,000
Southern Troops Involved: 18,000
Northern Casualties: 2,346
Southern Casualties: 2,534
Interesting Facts: This battle was actually two separate battles.

Crampton's Gap

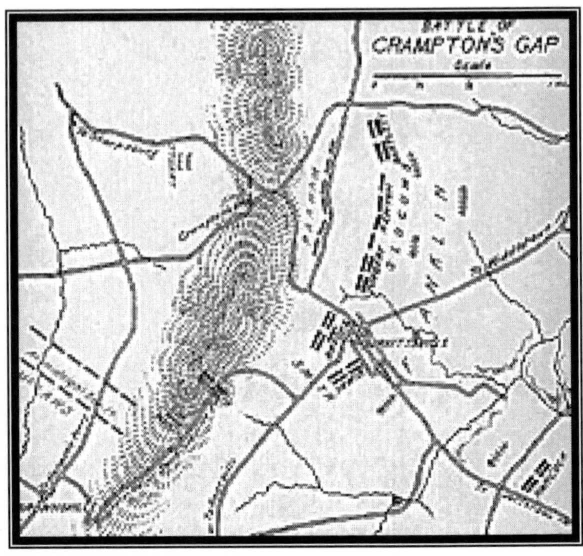

Northern Name for Battle: Crampton's Gap
Southern Name for Battle: Crampton's Gap
Location of Battle: Crampton's Gap, Maryland
Date of Battle: September 14, 1862
Northern Commander: Ambrose Everett Burnside and George Henry Thomas
Southern Commander: Robert E. Lee
Winner: Union
Northern Troops Involved: 12,800
Southern Troops Involved: 2,100
Northern Casualties: 3,750
Southern Casualties: 2,844
Interesting Facts: There were two other battles within five miles of this battle on the same day.

Corinth

Northern Name for Battle: Corinth
Southern Name for Battle: Corinth
Location of Battle: Alcorn County, Mississippi
Date of Battle: October 3-4, 1862
Northern Commander: William S. Rosecrans
Southern Commander: Earl Van Dorn
Winner: Union
Northern Troops Involved: 23,000
Southern Troops Involved: 22,000
Northern Casualties: 2,520
Southern Casualties: 9,233
Interesting Facts: The Confederates had to postpone their attack by several hours due to a sick commander.

Perryville

Northern Name for Battle: Perryville
Southern Name for Battle: Perryville
Location of Battle: Boyle County, Kentucky
Date of Battle: October 8, 1862
Northern Commander: Don Carlos Buell
Southern Commander: Braxton Bragg
Winner: Union
Northern Troops Involved: 36,940
Southern Troops Involved: 16,000
Northern Casualties: 4,211
Southern Casualties: 3,396
Interesting Facts: This battle started with a skirmish over drinking water.

Fredericksburg

Northern Name for Battle: Fredericksburg
Southern Name for Battle: Fredericksburg
Location of Battle: Spotsylvania County and Fredericksburg, Virginia
Date of Battle: December 13, 1862
Northern Commander: Ambrose Everett Burnside
Southern Commander: Robert E. Lee
Winner: Confederates
Northern Troops Involved: 114,000
Southern Troops Involved: 72,000
Northern Casualties: 12,653
Southern Casualties: 5,309
Interesting Facts: One of the most one-sided battles of the war.

Stones River

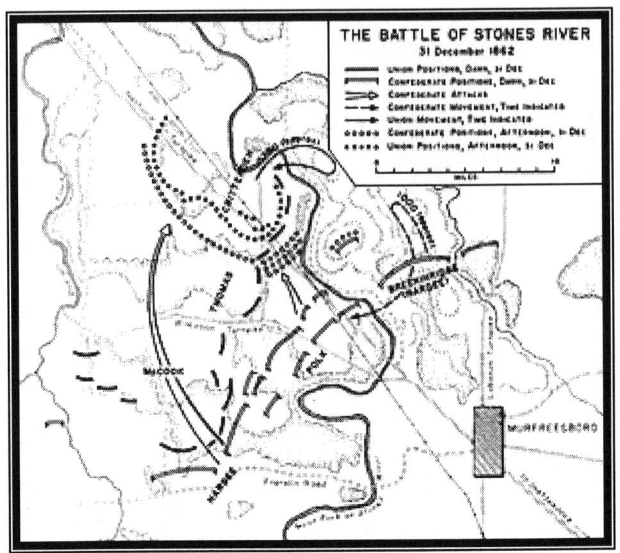

Northern Name for Battle: Stones River
Southern Name for Battle: Murfreesboro
Location of Battle: Stones River, Tennessee
Date of Battle: December 31, 1862
Northern Commander: William Starks Rosencrans
Southern Commander: Braxton Bragg
Winner: Union
Northern Troops Involved: 43,000
Southern Troops Involved: 37,000
Northern Casualties: 1,259
Southern Casualties: 10,266
Interesting Facts: This battle had the highest percentage of casualties on both sides during the war.

Chancellorsville

Northern Name for Battle: Chancellorsville
Southern Name for Battle: Chancellorsville
Location of Battle: Spotsylvania County, Virginia
Date of Battle: May 1-5 1863
Northern Commander: Joseph Hooker
Southern Commanders: Robert E. Lee
Winner: Confederates
Northern Troops Involved: 130,000
Southern Troops Involved: 57,352
Northern Casualties: 16,792
Southern Casualties: 12,764
Interesting Facts: The battle lasted 14 days, and was the third costliest battle of the Civil War.

Champion's Hill

Northern Name for Battle: Champion's Hill
Southern Name for Battle: Champion's Hill
Location of Battle: Hinds County, Mississippi
Date of Battle: May 16, 1863
Northern Commander: Ulysses S. Grant
Southern Commander: John C. Pemberton
Winner: Union
Northern Troops Involved: 29,000
Southern Troops Involved: 20,000
Northern Casualties: 2,441
Southern Casualties: 3,851
Interesting Facts: Pemberton decided to disobey orders and tired out his troops, so the confederates lost the battle.

Vicksburg

Northern Name for Battle: Vicksburg
Southern Name for Battle: Vicksburg
Location of Battle: Warren County, Mississippi
Date of Battle: May 18-July 4, 1863
Northern Commander: Ulysses S. Grant
Southern Commander: John C. Pemberton
Winner: Union
Northern Troops Involved: 75,000
Southern Troops Involved: 60,000
Northern Casualties: 8,873
Southern Casualties: 39,491
Interesting Facts: This battle lasted 46 days and ended on the 4th of July.

Port Hudson

Northern Name for Battle: Port Hudson
Southern Name for Battle: Port Hudson
Location of Battle: East Baton Rouge Parish and East Feliciana Parish, Louisiana
Date of Battle: May 29-July 9, 1863
Northern Commander: Nathan Banks
Southern Commander: Franklin Gardner
Winner: Union
Northern Troops Involved: 30,000
Southern Troops Involved: 6,500
Northern Casualties: 5,000
Southern Casualties: 7,208
Interesting Facts: This battle lasted over a month.

Brandy Station

Northern Name for Battle: Brandy Station
Southern Name for Battle: Brandy Station
Location of Battle: Culpeper County, Virginia
Date of Battle: June 13-15, 1863
Northern Commander: Alfred Pleasanton
Southern Commander: Jeb Stuart
Winner: Tie
Northern Troops Involved: 11,000
Southern Troops Involved: 9,500
Northern Casualties: 907
Southern Casualties: 523
Interesting Facts: From this point in the war, the union cavalry gained strength and confidence.

Second Winchester

Northern Name for Battle: Second Winchester
Southern Name for Battle: Second Winchester
Location of Battle: Frederick county and Winchester, VA.
Date of Battle: June 13-15 1863
Northern Commander: Robert Milroy
Southern Commander: Richard S. Ewell
Winner: Tie
Northern Troops Involved: 6,900
Southern Troops Involved: 12,500
Northern Casualties: 12,410
Southern Casualties: 13,724
Interesting Facts: This victory was the high point of Ewell's career.

Gettysburg

Northern Name for Battle: Gettysburg
Southern Name for Battle: Gettysburg
Location of Battle: Gettysburg, Pennsylvania
Date of Battle: July 1-3, 1863
Northern Commander: George Gordon Meade
Southern Commander: Robert E. Lee
Winner: Union
Northern Troops Involved: 83,000
Southern Troops Involved: 57,352
Northern Casualties: 23,049
Southern Casualties: 28,063
Interesting Facts: This was the bloodiest and possibly the most famous battle of the war. It was the "high water mark" of the Confederacy and began a losing streak for the South.

Chickamauga

Northern Name for Battle: Chickamauga
Southern Name for Battle: Chickamauga
Location of Battle: Catoosa County and Walker County, Georgia
Date of Battle: September 19-21, 1863
Northern Commander: George Henry Thomas
Southern Commander: Braxton Bragg
Winner: Confederates
Northern Troops Involved: 58,000
Southern Troops Involved: 68,000
Northern Casualties: 16,170
Southern Casualties: 18,454
Interesting Facts: This battle was the second costliest battle of the Civil War.

Chattanooga

Northern Name for Battle: Chattanooga
Southern Name for Battle: Chattanooga
Location of Battle: Hamilton County, Chattanooga City, Tennessee
Date of Battle: November 23-25, 1863
Northern Commander: Grant and Thomas
Southern Commander: Braxton Bragg
Winner: Union
Northern Troops Involved: 56,000
Southern Troops Involved: 46,000
Northern Casualties: 5,824
Southern Casualties: 6,667
Interesting Facts: After this battle the Union had complete control of Tennessee.

Mansfield

Northern Name for Battle: Mansfield
Southern Name for Battle: Mansfield
Location of Battle: DeSoto, Parish
Date of Battle: April 8, 1864
Northern Commander: Nathan Banks
Southern Commander: Richard Taylor
Winner: Confederates
Northern Troops Involved: unknown
Southern Troops Involved: unknown
Northern Casualties: 2,900
Southern Casualties: 1,500
Interesting Facts: This was the first major clash of the Union's Red River Campaign.

Wilderness

Northern Name for Battle: Wilderness
Southern Name for Battle: Wilderness
Location of Battle: Shadwell County, Virginia
Date of Battle: May 5-7, 1864
Northern Commander: Ulysses S. Grant
Southern Commander: Robert E. Lee
Winner: Undecided
Northern Troops Involved: 102,000
Southern Troops Involved: 61,000
Northern Casualties: 17,666
Southern Casualties: 7,750
Interesting Facts: More casualties were inflicted on the Union in this battle, but a higher percentage of casualties were inflicted on the South.

Spotsylvania

Northern Name for Battle: Spotsylvania
Southern Name for Battle: Spotsylvania
Location of Battle: Spotsylvania County, Virginia
Date of Battle: May 8-20, 1864
Northern Commander: Ulysses S. Grant
Southern Commander: Robert E. Lee
Winner: Tie
Northern Troops Involved: 100,000
Southern Troops Involved: 52,000
Northern Casualties: 18,399
Southern Casualties: 9,500
Interesting Facts: This battle was the fourth costliest battle of the Civil War.

Drewery's Bluff

Northern Name for Battle: Drewery's Bluff
Southern Name for Battle: Drewery's Bluff
Location of Battle:
Date of Battle: May 15, 1864
Northern Commander: John Rodgers
Southern Commander: Ebenezer Farrand
Winner: Tie
Northern Troops Involved:
Southern Troops Involved:
Northern Casualties: 24
Southern Casualties: 15
Interesting Facts: This battle had fewer than 40 casualties.

Resaca

Northern Name for Battle: Resaca
Southern Name for Battle: Resaca
Location of Battle: Gordon, and Whitman County, Georgia
Date of Battle: September 17, 1862
Northern Commander: Sherman
Southern Commander: J.E.Johnston
Winner: Tie
Northern Troops Involved: 98,787
Southern Troops Involved: 45,000
Northern Casualties: 2,747
Southern Casualties: 2,800
Interesting Facts: Johnston knew he couldn't win the battle, but he still made sure the Union forces had more casualties in the end.

Cold Harbor

Northern Name for Battle: Cold Harbor
Southern Name for Battle: Cold Harbor
Location of Battle: Hanover County, Virginia
Date of Battle: June 1-3, 1864
Northern Commanders: Ulysses S. Grant and George G. Meade
Southern Commander: Robert E. Lee
Winner: Confederate
Northern Troops Involved: 108,000
Southern Troops Involved: 62,000
Northern Casualties: 12,284
Southern Casualties: Unknown
Interesting Facts: After what became a slaughter of Union troops, Grant wrote in his memoirs that this was the only attack he wished he had not ordered.

Kearsarge Versus the Alabama

Northern Name for Battle: The Kearsarge Versus The Alabama
Southern Name for Battle: The Kearsarge Versus The Alabama
Location of Battle: Cherbough, France
Date of Battle: June 12, 1864
Northern Commander: John A. Winslow
Southern Commander: Raphael Seemes
Winner: Union
Northern Troops Involved: 162
Southern Troops Involved: 149
Northern Casualties: 3
Southern Casualties: 40
Interesting Facts: This battle was fought in France.

Petersburg

Northern Name for Battle: Petersburg
Southern Name for Battle: Petersburg
Location of Battle: Petersburg, Virginia
Date of Battle: June 15-18, 1864
Northern Commanders: Ulysses S. Grant and George G. Meade
Southern Commanders: Robert E. Lee and P.G.T. Beauregard
Winner: Confederates
Northern Troops Involved: 62,000
Southern Troops Involved: 42,000
Northern Casualties: 8,150
Southern Casualties: Unknown
Interesting Facts: This battle was actually a ten month siege.

Kennesaw Mountain

Northern Name for Battle: Kennesaw Mountain
Southern Name for Battle: Kennesaw Mountain
Location of Battle: Kennesaw, Georgia
Date of Battle: June 27, 1864
Northern Commander: William T. Sherman
Southern Commander: Joseph E. Johnston
Winner: Confederate
Northern Troops Involved: 100,000
Southern Troops Involved: 50,000
Northern Casualties: 2,051
Southern Casualties: 442
Interesting Facts: Not much of the battle was actually fought on Kennesaw Mountain.

Atlanta

Northern Name for Battle: Atlanta
Southern Name for Battle: Atlanta
Location of Battle: Fulton County, Georgia
Date of Battle: July 22, 1864
Northern Commanders: William T. Sherman, James B. McPherson
Southern Commander: John B. Hood
Winner: Union
Northern Troops Involved: 30,000
Southern Troops Involved: 37,000
Northern Casualties: 3,722
Southern Casualties: 8,500
Interesting Facts: Another general, Hardee forgot where he was supposed to go, so the South lost the battle.

The Crater

Northern Name for Battle: The Crater
Southern Name for Battle: The Crater
Location of Battle:
Date of Battle: July 30, 1864
Northern Commander: Ambrose Everet Burnside
Southern Commander: Robert E. Lee
Winner: Confederate
Northern Troops Involved: unknown
Southern Troops Involved: unknown
Northern Casualties: 3,789
Southern Casualties: 1,491
Interesting Facts: This battle was called the crater because the troops blew up 8,000 pounds of gunpowder 20 feet under the Confederate troops, creating a huge crater.

Mobile Bay

Northern Name for Battle: Mobile Bay
Southern Name for Battle: Mobile Bay
Location of Battle: Mobile County, Baldwin County, Alabama
Date of Battle: August 2-23, 1864
Northern Commanders: David G. Farragut and Gordon Granger
Southern Commanders: Franklin Buchanan and Richard L. Page
Winner: Union
Northern Troops Involved: 14 wooden ships, four ironclad monitors, and several gunboats
Southern Troops Involved: 3 gunboats and 1 ironclad
Northern Casualties: 322
Southern Casualties: 1,500
Interesting Facts: There were five ironclads used in this battle.

Globe Tavern

Northern Name for Battle: Globe Tavern
Southern Name for Battle: Globe Tavern
Location of Battle: Dinwiddie County, Virginia
Date of Battle: August 18-21, 1864
Northern Commander: Warren
Southern Commander: Lee
Winner: Union
Troops Involved: 34,300
Northern Casualties: 4,279
Southern Casualties: 1,600
Interesting Facts: This was the Union army's first decisive battle of the siege of Petersburg.

Third Winchester

Northern Name for Battle: Third Winchester
Southern Name for Battle: Third Winchester
Location of Battle: Winchester, Virginia
Date of Battle: September 19, 1864
Northern Commander: Sheridan
Southern Commander: Early
Winner: Union
Northern Troops Involved:
Southern Troops Involved:
Northern Casualties: 5,020
Southern Casualties: 3,610
Interesting Facts: This was the third battle fought on this site.

Cedar Creek

Northern Name for Battle: Cedar Creek
Southern Name for Battle: Cedar Creek
Location of Battle: Frederick County, Shenandoah, Warren County, Virginia
Date of Battle: October 19, 1864
Northern Commanders: Horatio Wright and Philip Sheridan
Southern Commander: Jubal Early
Winner: Union
Northern Troops Involved: 31,945
Southern Troops Involved: 21,000
Northern Casualties: 5,665
Southern Casualties: 2,910
Interesting Facts: Sheridan wasn't at the battle when it started. He was coming back from a conference in Washington, and both commanders received much more credit and blame than they should have.

Franklin

Northern Name for Battle: Franklin
Southern Name for Battle: Franklin
Location of Battle: William County, Tennessee
Date of Battle: November 30, 1864
Northern Commander: John M. Schofield
Southern Commander: John B. Hood
Winner: Union
Northern Troops Involved: 28,000
Southern Troops Involved: 27,000
Northern Casualties: 2,326
Southern Casualties: 6,252
Interesting Facts: This battle was called the bloodiest hour of the war.

Fort McAllister

Northern Name for Battle: Fort McAllister
Southern Name for Battle: Fort McAllister
Location of Battle: Bryon County, Georgia
Date of Battle: Shadwell, Virginia
Northern Commander: William B. Hazen
Southern Commander: George A. Anderson
Winner: Union
Northern Troops Involved: 62,000
Southern Troops Involved: 120
Northern Casualties: 134
Southern Casualties: 93
Interesting Facts: This battle only lasted 15 to 20 minutes.

Nashville

Northern Name for Battle: Nashville
Southern Name for Battle: Nashville
Location of Battle: Nashville, Tennessee
Date of Battle: December 15-16, 1864
Northern Commander: George H. Thomas
Southern Commander: John Bell Hood
Winner: Union
Northern Troops Involved: 50,000
Southern Troops Involved: 23,000
Northern Casualties: 3,061
Southern Casualties: 5,962
Interesting Facts: This battle started two weeks after both armies arrived in Nashville.

Bentonville

Northern Name for Battle: Bentonville
Southern Name for Battle: Bentonville
Location of Battle: Bentonville, North Carolina
Date of Battle: March 19-21, 1865
Northern Commander: Sherman
Southern Commander: J.E. Johnston
Winner: Union
Northern Troops Involved: 30,000
Southern Troops Involved: 20,000
Northern Casualties: 1,646
Southern Casualties: 2,606
Interesting Facts: This was one of the last major engagements of the Civil War

Final Petersburg

Northern Name for Battle: Final Petersburg
Southern Name for Battle: Final Petersburg
Location of Battle: Petersburg, Virginia
Date of Battle: April 2, 1865
Northern Commander: Grant
Southern Commander: Lee
Winner: Tie
Northern Troops Involved: 97,000
Southern Troops Involved: 45,000
Northern Casualties: 12,410
Southern Casualties: 13,724
Interesting Facts: This battle ended a ten month siege of Petersburg.

Sailor's Creek

Northern Name for Battle: Sailor's Creek
Southern Name for Battle: Sailor's Creek
Location of Battle: Sailor's Creek, Virginia
Date of Battle: April 6, 8165
Northern Commander: Sheridan
Southern Commander: Ewell
Winner: Union
Northern Troops Involved: unknown
Southern Troops Involved: unknown
Northern Casualties: 1,180
Southern Casualties: 7,000
Interesting Facts: Nearly one fourth of the Confederate troops were cut off during their retreat.

Appomattox Courthouse

Northern Name for Battle: Appomattox Courthouse
Southern Name for Battle: Appomattox Courthouse
Location of Battle: Appomattox Courthouse, Virginia
Date of Battle: April 9, 1865
Northern Commander: Ulysses S. Grant
Southern Commander: Robert E. Lee
Winner: Union
Northern Troops Involved: 120,000
Southern Troops Involved: 30,000
Northern Casualties: 260
Southern Casualties: 440
Interesting Facts: General Lee surrenders, effectively ending the war.

Palmetto Ranch

Northern Name for Battle: Palmetto Ranch
Southern Name for Battle: Palmetto Ranch
Location of Battle: Palmetto Ranch, Texas
Date of Battle: May 12-13,1865
Northern Commander: Theodore Barrett
Southern Commander: John Ford
Winner: Confederate
Northern Troops Involved: unknown
Southern Troops Involved: unknown
Northern Casualties: 118
Southern Casualties: Unknown
Interesting Facts: The war was nearly over in every other state but was still going on in Texas, resulting in this battle.

Number of Battles of the Civil War by State

Alabama	78
Arizona	4
Arkansas	167
California	6
Colorado	4
Dakota Territory	11
District of Columbia	1
Florida	32
Georgia	108
Idaho	1
Illinois	1
Indian Territory (now part of Oklahoma)	17
Indiana	4
Kansas	7
Kentucky	138
Louisiana	118
Maine	1
Maryland	30
Minnesota	6

Mississippi	186
Missouri	244
Nebraska	2
Nevada	2
New Mexico	19
New York	1
North Carolina	85
Ohio	3
Oregon	4
Pennsylvania	9
South Carolina	60
Tennessee	298
Texas	14
Utah	1
Virginia	519
Washington Territory	1
West Virginia	80
TOTAL	**2262**

Battles With Dual Names

There is a difference of opinion when it comes to naming some of the battles, even today. The Northern forces often named battles after rivers or creeks, while Southern forces often named them after nearby towns. In fact, the Civil War itself was known by multitude of different names. A few of the dual-named battles are listed here.

Northern Name	Southern Name
Bull Run	Manassas
Wilson's Creek	Oak Hills
Ball's Bluff	Leesburg
Logan's Cross Roads	Mill Springs
Pea Ridge	Elkhorn Tavern
Pittsburg Landing	Shiloh
Seven Pines	Fair Oaks
Chickahominy River	Gaine's Mill
Chantilly	Ox Hill
South Mountain	Boonsboro
Antietam	Sharpsburg
Chaplin Hills	Perryville
Stones River	Murfreesboro
Sabine Cross Roads	Mansfield
Opequon	Winchester

Northern Military Leaders

Adlebert Ames

Full Name: Adlebert Ames
Born: October 31, 1835
Place of Birth: Rockland, Maine
North or South: North
Education: Graduated West Point, 1861
Pre-War Profession: Sailor
Post-War Profession: Army service, provisional governor of Mississippi, resigned US Army 1870, US senator, state governor, Spanish-American War.
War Service Highlights: He commanded the 2nd Division XXIV Corps.
Nickname: None
Died: April 13, 1933
Place of Death: Ormand, Florida
Interesting Facts: Post-war political activities marred his good war record. He was a governor in the United States.

William Averell

Full Name: William Woods Averell
Born: November 5, 1832
Place of Birth: Cameron, New York
North or South: North
Education: Graduated West Point, 1855
Pre-War Profession: Drug clerk, garrison duty, frontier service, injured from 1859 to 1861.
Post-War Profession: US consul general in Montreal, inventor.
War Service Highlights: He commanded 2nd Cavalry Division in Sheridan's Shenandoah Valley campaign.
Nickname: None
Died: February 3, 1900
Place of Death: Bath, New York
Interesting Facts: After he graduated, he fought against Native Americans in the Southwest, and was recovering from battle wounds when the Civil War began. In 1861 he carried messages to the U.S. Army.

Nathaniel Banks

Full Name: Nathaniel Prentiss Banks
Born: January 30, 1816
Place of Birth: Waltham, Massachusetts
North or South: North
Education: Unknown
Pre-War Profession: Cotton mill worker, lawyer, politician, US congressman, House Speaker, state governor.
Post-War Profession: US congressman, US marshal.
War Service Highlights: He was the commander of the Department of the Gulf.
Nickname: "Commissary Banks"
Died: September 1, 1894
Place of Death: Waltham, Massachusetts
Interesting Facts: He served under five different parties during his political career.

Don Carlos Buell

Full Name: Don Carlos Buell
Born: March 23, 1818
Place of Birth: Lowell, Ohio
North or South: north
Education: Graduate of West Point in 1841.
Pre-War Profession: Fought Indians in Florida, garrison and frontier duty, Mexican war, staff duties.
Post-War Profession: President of an ironworks, pension agent.
War Service Highlights: He led the Army of the Ohio.
Nickname: None
Died: November 19, 1898
Place of Death: Paradise, Kentucky
Interesting Facts: Regarded as overly cautious.

Ambrose Burnside

Full Name: Ambrose Everett Burnside
Born: May 23, 1824
Place of Birth: Liberty, Illinois
North or South: North
Education: West Point graduate of 1847.
Pre-War Profession: Tailor, Mexican war, frontier duty, resigned U.S. Army 1853, businessman, militia officer.
Post-War Profession: Governor, businessman, U.S. senator.
War Service Highlights: He commanded a brigade at First Bull Run.
Nickname: None
Died: September 13, 1881
Place of Death: Bristol, Rhode Island
Interesting Facts: He was an unwilling commander of the Army of the Potomac.

Benjamin Butler

Full Name: Benjamin Franklin Butler
Born: November 5, 1818
Place of Birth: Deerfield, New Hampshire
North or South: North
Education: Graduated from Waterville College in 1838.
Pre-War Profession: Teacher, lawyer, politician
Post-War Profession: Us Congressman, Governor, Presidential Candidate
War Service Highlights: He commanded Army of the James.
Nickname: "Beast" & "Spoons"
Died: January 11, 1893
Place of Death: Washington D.C.
Interesting Facts: A controversial political general, notorious for his use of contraband slaves and his disrespect towards the ladies of New Orleans.

Kit Carson

Full Name: Christopher Carson
Born: December 24, 1809
Place of Birth: Kentucky
North or South: North
Education: none
Pre-War Profession: Fur trapper, army scout, buffalo hunter
Post-War Profession: None
War Service Highlights: Carson organized and commanded the New Mexico and Colorado Auxiliary Scouts. At the end of the war he was appointed to the rank of Brigadier General and given command of Fort Garland, Colorado. Christopher Carson left the post in 1867 and died at Fort Lyons in 1868.
Nickname: "Kit"
Died: April, 1868
Place of Death: Boggsville, Colorado
Interesting Facts: When he was an infant his parents immigrated to what is now Howard County, Missouri. He was a very modest man and never boasted about his achievements.

Joshua Chamberlain

Full Name: Joshua Lawrence Chamberlain
Born: September 8, 1828
Place of Birth: Brewer, Maine
North or South: North
Education: none
Pre-War Profession: College professor
Post-War Profession: Governor, college president, businessman, author.
War Service Highlights: He commanded the 20th Maine.
Nickname: none
Died: February 24, 1914
Place of Death: Portland, Maine
Interesting Facts: Led the critical bayonet charge on the Union left on Little Round Top.

George Crook

Full Name: George Crook
Born: September 8, 1828
Place of Birth: Dayton, Ohio
North or South: North
Education: Graduated West Point. 1852.
Pre-War Profession: Duty in Pacific Northwest.
Post-War Profession: Army service as Indian fighter, commanded the Division of the Missouri.
War Service Highlights: He commanded a division of cavalry in Army of the Potomac in Appomattox campaign.
Nickname: None
Died: March 21, 1890
Place of Death: Chicago, Illinois
Interesting Facts: He spent the first part of his military career in Northern California and Oregon.

George Custer

Full Name: George Armstrong Custer
Born: December 5, 1839
Place of Birth: Harrison City, Ohio
North or South: North
Education: Graduated from West Point 1861
Pre-War Profession: Teacher
Post-War Profession: Army service as an Indian fighter, publicist.
War Service Highlights: He commanded the Fifth Cavalry Division in the Shenandoah Valley campaign.
Nickname: "Auntie", "Fanny", "Curly"
Died: June 25, 1876
Place of Death: Little Big Horn, Montana
Interesting Facts: He became the youngest general in the Union army at age 23.

Abner Doubleday

Full Name: Abner Doubleday
Born: June 26, 1819
Place of Birth: Ballston Spa, New York
North or South: North
Education: West Point graduate of 1842.
Pre-War Profession: Seminole wars, Mexican war.
Post-War Profession: Army service, fought Indians, retired in 1886
War Service Highlights: He commanded First Corps at Gettysburg after Reynolds fell.
Nickname: None
Died: January 26, 1893
Place of Death: Mendham, New Jersey
Interesting Facts: He is incorrectly credited with originating the game of baseball.

Ulysses S. Grant

Full Name: Ulysses Simpson Grant
Born: April 27, 1822
Place of Birth: Point Pleasant, Ohio
North or South: North
Education: West Point, 1843
Pre-War Profession: Mexican war, garrison duty, resigned 1854, firewood peddler, store clerk.
Post-War Profession: Army service, US president, businessman, writer.
War Service Highlights: He commanded the Army of the Tennessee and eventually became commander of all Union forces.
Nickname: Uncle Sam
Died: July 23, 1885
Place of Death: Mount McGregor, New York
Interesting Facts: He had a big variety of jobs in the Mid West. Ulysses was a Republican candidate for president. He was in the election with Horatio Seymour. He won the election, and he ran for president again in 1872. He won that election against Horace Greeley, a Democratic. After he retired from office he toured Europe for two years.

Henry Halleck

Full Name: Henry Wager Halleck
Born: January 16, 1815
Place of Birth: Westernville, New York
North or South: North
Education: Graduated West Point, 1839
Pre-War Profession: Instructor at West Point, author, Mexican War, Secretary of State of California, lawyer
Post-War Profession: Army service, commanded in dept. of the Pacific and the South.
War Service Highlights: He was the commander of the Department of the Missouri.
Nickname: None
Died: January 9, 1872
Place of Death: Louisville, Kentucky
Interesting Facts: He was an effective administrator, but a poor field commander.

Winfield Scott Hancock

Full Name: Winfield Scott Hancock
Born: February 14, 1824
Place of Birth: Montgomery Square, Pennsylvania
North or South: North
Education: Graduated West Point, 1844
Pre-War Profession: Instructor at West Point, Frontier Duty, Mexican War, Kansas War, Utah Expedition, Quartermaster Service.
Post-War Profession: Army service, Commanded Dept of the East, U.S. presidential candidate, 1880.
War Service Highlights: He commanded Second Corps at Gettysburg.
Nickname: None
Died: February 9, 1872
Place of Death: Governor's Island, New York
Interesting Facts: Was considered one of the greatest eastern generals. He was one of the best Corps Commanders for the Union army. People wanted him as their president, in the US, but he lost to James Garfield.

Joseph Hooker

Full Name: Joseph Hooker
Born: November 13, 1814
Place of Birth: Hadley, Massachusetts
North or South: He was a northern general.
Education: Graduate of West Point in 1837.
Pre-War Profession: Seminole War, adjutant at West Point, involved in the Mexican War, resigned from the U.S army in 1853, farmer, served in California state militia.
Post-War Profession: Hooker was in the army service, he retired from the army service in 1868 due to invalidity.
War Service Highlights: He commanded Army of the Potomac at Chancellorsville.
Nickname: None
Died: October 31, 1879
Place of Death: Garden City, New York
Interesting Facts: He restored his reputation somewhat by his good leadership on Lookout Mountain and in the Atlanta campaign.

Oliver Howard

Full Name: Oliver Otis Howard
Born: November 8, 1830
Place of Birth: Leeward, Maine
North or South: North
Education: Graduated West Point 1854
Pre-War Profession: Mathematics teacher at West Point
Post-War Profession: Head of Freeman's Bureau, helped establish Howard University, fought Indians, superintendent at West Point, commanded Division of the East, retired 1894, Educator.
War Service Highlights: He commanded Army of the Tennessee in March to the Sea.
Nickname: None
Died: October 26, 1909
Place of Death: Burlington, Vermont
Interesting Facts: He was a Christian soldier. He was also a writer and many liked his books. He was a brave warrior in the Civil War who did many things to help slaves. He created a bank and a school for blacks.

David Hunter

Full Name: David Hunter
Born: July 21, 1802
Place of Birth: District of Columbia
North or South: North
Education: Graduated West Point, 1822
Pre-War Profession: Frontier duty.
Post-War Profession: Army service, presided over the commission that tried the conspirators in Lincoln's assassination, retired 1866.
War Service Highlights: He commanded Department of West Virginia.
Nickname: None
Died: February 2, 1886
Place of Death: Washington, D.C.
Interesting Facts: His defeat in the Shenandoah Valley left the way open for Early's Washington raid.

Hugh Kilpatrick

Full Name: Hugh Judson Kilpatrick
Born: January 14, 1836
Place of Birth: Deckertown, New Jersey
North or South: North
Education: Graduated West Point, 1861
Pre-War Profession: None
Post-War Profession: U.S. Minister to Chile
War Service Highlights: He commanded the cavalry in the Atlanta campaign.
Nickname: Kill Cavalry
Died: December 4, 1881
Place of Death: Santiago, Chile
Interesting Facts: Goaded Elon Foarsworth to make his unnecessary charge on Gettysburg.

George McClellan

Full Name: George Brinton McClellan
Born: December 3, 1826
Place of Birth: Philadelphia, Pennsylvania
North or South: North
Education: Graduated West Point, 1846
Pre-War Profession: Duty in Engineers, Mexican War, constructed forts and harbors, instructor at West Point, observer in Crimean War, saddle designer, resigned US army 1857, railroad executive.
Post-War Profession: Civil engineer, businessman, author, Governor of New Jersey.
War Service Highlights: He commanded the Army of the Potomac.
Nickname: None
Died: October 29, 1885
Place of Death: Orange, New Jersey
Interesting Facts: He organized the Army of the Potomac brilliantly, but was reluctant to use it to fight.

Irvin McDowell

Full Name: Irvin McDowell
Born: October 15, 1885
Place of Birth: Columbus, Ohio
North or South: North
Education: Graduated West Point, 1838
Pre-War Profession: Instructor at West Point, Mexican War, Staff officer.
Post-War Profession: Army service, commanded Depts. in the South and West, retired 1882.
War Service Highlights: He commanded the Third Corps at Second Bull Run.
Nickname: None
Died: May 4, 1885
Place of Death: San Francisco, California
Interesting Facts: He received his early education in France. He was not known for his performance as a general, he was criticized for it. The Battle of Bull Run was a tough battle to give up for McDowell but his troops were no match for experienced Confederate troops.

George Meade

Full Name: George Gordon Meade
Born: December 31, 1815
Place of Birth: Cadiz, Spain
North or South: North
Education: Graduated West Point, 1835
Pre-War Profession: Seminole War, ordnance duty, resigned US Army 1836, railroad engineering work, surveyor, rejoined army 1842, survey duty, Mexican war, engineering duty.
War Service Highlights: He commanded the Army of the Potomac from Gettysburg onward.
Post-War Profession: Army service, commanded Military Division of the Atlantic and Department of the East, Reconstruction administration.
Nickname: None
Died: November 6, 1872
Place of Death: Philadelphia, Pennsylvania
Interesting Facts: He was born in Spain.

Galusha Pennypacker

Full Name: Galusha Pennypacker
Born: June 1, 1844
Place of Birth: Chester City, PA
North or South: North
Education: Unknown
Pre-War Profession: He was a student.
Post-War Profession: Army service, frontier duty, retired 1883.
War Service Highlights: He was a Brigadier General of Volunteers and he was in the 97th Pennsylvania.
Nickname: None
Died: October 1, 1916
Place of Death: Philadelphia, Pennsylvania
Interesting Facts: There is some evidence that he wasn't born in 1844 and born in 1842 instead.

Alfred Pleasanton

Full Name: Alfred Pleasanton
Born: July 7, 1824
Place of Birth: District of Columbia
North or South: North
Education: Graduated West Point, 1844
Pre-War Profession: Mexican War, Frontier Duty
Post-War Profession: Army service resigned in 1868.
War Service Highlights: He commanded the Cavalry Corps at Brandy Station and in the Gettysburg campaign.
Nickname: None
Died: February 17, 1897
Place of Death: District of Columbia
Interesting Facts: He ended the last Confederate threat in the west.

John Pope

Full Name: John Pope
Born: March 16, 1822
Place of Birth: Louisville, Kentucky
North or South: North
Education: West Point graduate of 1842.
Pre-War Profession: He was in the Mexican War, engineering and topographical duty.
Post-War Profession: Army service, fought Indians, retired in 1886.
War Service Highlights: He commanded the Army of Virginia at Second Bull Run.
Nickname: None
Died: September 23, 1892
Place of Death: Sandusky, Ohio
Interesting Facts: Pope was blamed for losing the battle of Bull Run by many. Because of this, he was not employed again until 1882, when he was returned to the rank of major general.

Fitz John Porter

Full Name: Fitz John Porter
Born: August 31, 1822
Place of Birth: Portsmouth, New Hampshire
North or South: North
Education: Graduate of West Point, 1845.
Pre-War Profession: Mexican War, artillery instructor at West Point, Utah Expedition.
Post-War Profession: The court martial was politically inspired by Edward Stanton, to harm George McClellan. Porter fought to clear his name, and was exonerated in 1878.
War Service Highlights: He commanded the Fifth Corps in Seven Days.
Nickname: None
Died: May 21, 1901
Place of Death: Morristown, New Jersey
Interesting Facts: He was liked by many of his men, but he was blamed for Pope's defeat.

William Rosencrans

Full Name: William Starke Rosencrans
Born: September 6, 1819
Place of Birth: Delaware City, Ohio
North or South: North
Education: Graduate of West Point in 1842.
Pre-War Profession: Engineer Duty, resigned US Army 1854, architect, civil engineer.
Post-War Profession: Army service, March 1861 Brigadier General in Confederate Provisional Army, Fort Sumter, First Manassas, July 1861 General, Shiloh - commanded Army of Tennessee after A. S. Johnston killed, Corinth, superseded by Bragg while on sick leave, defense of South Carolina and Georgia, commanded defenses south of Richmond, second in command to Johnston in Carolinas campaign.
War Service Highlights: He was the commander of the Army of Mississippi.
Nickname: "Old Rosey"
Died: March 11, 1898
Place of Death: Redondo, California
Interesting Facts: A very poor field commander, who was saved at Chickamauga by Thomas's stand, and allowed himself to be besieged at Chattanooga. However, his Tullahoma campaign was a strategic success.

Alexander Schimmelfennig

Full Name: Alexander Schimmelfennig
Born: July 20, 1824
Place of Birth: Lithauen, Prussia
North or South: North
Education: None
Pre-War Profession: Officer in Prussian Army, emigrated to US in 1853, writer, engineer, draftsman.
Post-War Profession: None
War Service Highlights: He commanded the 74th Pennsylvania.
Nickname: "Schimmel"
Died: September 5, 1865
Place of Death: Wernersvillem, Pennsylvania
Interesting Facts: Although born a Junker, he was a devoted socialist and changed his name from Von Schimmelfennig. Contracted tuberculosis around the end of the war.

Winfield Scott

Full Name: Winfield Scott
Born: June 13, 1786
Place of Birth: Petersburg Virginia
North or South: North
Other Professions: Fought in every war from 1812, commander in chief of the Army. Wrote memoirs, travelled.
War Service: 1861 Major General (since 1841), Union commander in chief, conceived the "Anaconda Plan", retired October 1861 after McClellan was made commander of the Army of the Potomac.
Nickname: "Old Fuss and Feathers"
Died: May 29, 1866
Place of Death: West Point, New York
Interesting Facts: Scott ran against Franklin Pierce for president but lost. In 1856 he received a brevet promotion to the rank of a lieutenant general. Because of this he became the first American since George Washington to hold this rank!

John Sedgwick

Full Name: John Sedgwick
Born: September 13, 1813
Place of Birth: Cornwall Hollow, CT
North or South: North
Education: West Point graduate of 1837.
Pre-War Profession: He was a teacher who was involved in the Mexican War, cavalry duty, and frontier duty.
Post-War Profession: None
War Service Highlights: He commanded the Sixth Corps at Chancellorsville.
Nickname: "Uncle John"
Died: May 9, 1864
Place of Death: Spotsylvania, Virginia
Interesting Facts: Sedgwick was insulting the Confederates by saying that they "couldn't hit an elephant at a this distance", while he was in the battle of Spotsylvania. One second later a sniper's bullet hit him right under his left eye, killing him.

William Seward Jr.

Full Name: William Henry Seward Jr.
Born: June 18, 1839
Place of Birth: Auburn, New York
North or South: North
Education: None
Pre-War Profession: Store clerk, secretary to his father when he was a U.S. Senator, banker
Post-War Profession: Banker, businessman
War Service Highlights: He commanded a brigade in West Virginia.
Nickname: None
Died: April 26, 1920
Place of Death: Auburn, New York
Interesting Facts: He was the son of Secretary of State, William H. Seward.

Phillip Sheridan

Full Name: Phillip Henry Sheridan
Born: March 6, 1831
Place of Birth: Albany, New York
North or South: North
Education: Graduated from West Point in 1853
Pre-War Profession: Frontier Duty, Indian Fighter
Post-War Profession: Army service, commanded in the Military Division of the Gulf, commanded Fifth Military District, succeeded Sherman as commander-in-chief, author.
War Service Highlights: He commanded Cavalry of Army of the Potomac in Overland campaign.
Nickname: None
Died: August 5, 1888
Place of Death: Nosquitt, Massachusetts
Interesting Facts: His wife loved him so much that when he died she said "I would rather be the widow of Phil Sheridan than the wife of any man living."

William Tecumseh Sherman

Full Name: William Tecumseh Sherman
Born: February 8, 1820
Place of Birth: Lancaster, Ohio
North or South: North
Education: Graduated West Point, 1840.
Pre-War Profession: Artillery Duty, traveled widely in the south, Mexican war, served in Pacific division, resigned US army 1853, banker, lawyer, realtor, superintendent of Louisiana Military Academy.
Post-War Profession: Army service, Commanded the division of the Mississippi, Indian Campaign, General in Chief after Grant's election to presidency, retired 1883, author.
War Service Highlights: He commanded 5th Division/Army of the Tennessee at Shiloh.
Nickname: "Cump"
Died: February 14, 1891
Place of Death: New York, New York
Interesting Facts: He was a fierce commander, hated in the south, but had a vision of modern war.

Daniel Sickles

Full Name: Daniel Edgar Sickles
Born: October 20, 1819
Place of Birth: New York, New York
North or South: North
Other Professions: He was a patent lawyer and a politician.
War Service Highlights: General Sickles fought at Sharpsburg in Joseph Hooker's Division of III Corps. He also commanded a Division at Fredericksburg.
Nickname: None
Died: May 3, 1914
Place of Death: New York, New York
Interesting Facts: In a battle he got hit by a cannonball in the leg. They amputated his leg and put it in a museum. Every year on the anniversary, he went and visited his leg at the museum. Sickles was also the only General who fought at Gettysburg that was later captured on motion picture film. He was also the first person to use the insanity defense to escape a murder conviction.

Franz Sigel

Full Name: Franz Sigel
Born: November 18, 1824
Place of Birth: Baden, Germany
North or South: North
Education: Graduate of the German Military Academy.
Pre-War Profession: German army officer, revolutionary, emigrated to US, teacher.
Post-War Profession: Journalist, pension agent.
War Service Highlights: He commanded First Corps at Second Bull Run.
Nickname: None
Died: August 21, 1902
Place of Death: New York, New York
Interesting Facts: He resigned from the German army in 1847 and became involved in radical politics. He took part in the German Revolution in 1848, and was forced to go to Switzerland after that. He commanded the 4th Brigade of the Army of Southwest Missouri from January to February, 1862.

Edwin Stanton

Full Name: Edwin M. Stanton
Born: December 19, 1814
Place of Birth: Steubenville, Ohio
North or South: North
Education: Kenyon College 1833, studied law under a judge.
Pre-War Profession: Lawyer, politician
Post-War Profession: None
War Service Highlights: Secretary of War
Nickname: None
Died: December 24, 1869
Place of Death: Washington, DC
Interesting Facts: In his childhood, he suffered from asthma. He was a great politician who served the Union well.

Edwin Sumner

Full Name: Edwin Vose Sumner
Born: January 30, 1797
Place of Birth: Boston, Massachusetts
North or South: North
Education: Unknown
Pre-War Profession: Commissioned 2nd Lieutenant in US Army 1819, frontier duty, Mexican war, governor of New Mexico Territory, commanded Department of the West.
Post-War Profession: None
War Service Highlights: He commanded Second Corps in Peninsula campaign.
Nickname: "Bull Head"
Died: March 21, 1863
Place of Death: Syracuse, New York
Interesting Facts: He was the oldest general in the Civil War.

George Thomas

Full Name: George Henry Thomas
Born: July 31, 1816
Place of Birth: Southampton City, Virginia
North or South: North
Education: Graduated West Point, 1840
Pre-War Profession: Served in the artillery, Seminole war, Mexican war, instructor in Cavalry and Artillery at West Point, frontier duty in the 2nd US Cavalry.
Post-War Profession: Army service, commanded Division of the Pacific.
War Service Highlights: He commanded Army of the Cumberland at Chattanooga.
Nickname: "Pap"
Died: March 28, 1870
Place of Death: San Francisco, California
Interesting Facts: Despite Grant's poor opinion of him and general suspicion of his Southern sympathies, he was a fine commander.

Gouverneur Warren

Full Name: Gouverneur Kemble Warren
Born: January 18, 1830
Place of Birth: Cold Spring, New York
North or South: North
Education: Graduated West Point, 1850
Pre-War Profession: Engineering duty, Instructor at West Point
Post-War Profession: Army Service in Engineers, writer, railroad bridge builder.
War Service Highlights: He was the chief engineer of the Army of the Potomac at Gettysburg.
Nickname: None
Died: August 8, 1882
Place of Death: Newport, Rhode Island
Interesting Facts: Exonerated in 1882 by a court of inquiry, which criticized Sheridan's actions in relieving him.

James Wilson

Full Name: James Harrison Wilson
Born: September 2, 1837
Place of Birth: Shawneetown, Illinois
North or South: North
Education: Graduated West Point, 1860
Pre-War Profession: Assistant topographic engineer in Oregon.
Post-War Profession: Army service in the infantry and the engineers, discharged 1870 at his own request, writer, railroad manager, served as Major General of Volunteers in Puerto Rico and Cuba during Spanish-American War, Boxer Rebellion, US representative to Edward VII's coronation.
War Service Highlights: He commanded 3rd Division/Cavalry Corps for Richmond campaign.
Nickname: None
Died: February 23, 1925
Place of Death: Wilmington, Delaware
Interesting Facts: Probably the most distinguished of the "boy generals". He was the only officer promoted to troop command from Grant's regular staff.

John Wool

Full Name: John Ellis Wool
Born: February 29, 1784
Place of Birth: Newburgh, New York
North or South: North
Education: Unknown
Pre-War Profession: He was in the war of 1812, later he became a Brig. General USA, he moved the Cherokee Indians to eastern Oklahoma, involved in the Mexican War, commander of the Department of the East and Department of the Pacific.
Post-War Profession: None
War Service Highlights: On August 1861, he sent reinforcements to Fort Monroe to save it for the Union. He was promoted to Major General in the Regular Army on May 1862. He commanded the Middle Department and Department of the East, and later retired in August 1863.
Nickname: None
Died: November 10, 1869
Place of Death: Troy, New York
Interesting Facts: John was the oldest officer to exercise active command on either side in the Civil War.

Southern Military Leaders

Edward Alexander

Full Name: Edward Porter Alexander
Born: May 26, 1835
Place of Birth: Washington, Georgia
North or South: South
Education: Graduated from West Point, 1857
Pre-War Profession: Instructor at West Point, Utah expedition.
Post-War Profession: Professor of Engineering, railroad president, wrote memoirs.
War Service Highlights: He was chief of artillery in Longstreet's Corps.
Nickname: None
Died: April 28, 1910
Place of Death: Savannah, Georgia
Interesting Facts: Commanded the barrage before Pickett's charge.

Richard Anderson

Full Name: Richard Heron Anderson
Born: October 7, 1821
Place of Birth: Sumter City, South Carolina
North or South: South
Education: Graduated West Point, 1842.
Pre-War Profession: 2nd dragoons, Mexican War, resigned December 1860.
Post-War Profession: State phosphate agent.
War Service Highlights: When the Civil War began in 1861, Richard Heron Anderson resigned from the U.S. Army and entered the Confederate service as a brigadier general. Promoted to major general on July 14, 1862, Anderson fought at the Second Battle of Bull Run, Antietam, Fredericksburg, Gettysburg, Spotsylvania, and Cold Harbor. In May of 1864 Anderson was promoted to lieutenant general serving under General Robert E. Lee.
Nickname: "Fightin' Dick"
Died: June 6, 1879
Place of Death: Beaufort, South Carolina
Interesting Facts: Won the brevet of first lieutenant in the Mexican War in 1848 and captain in 1855.

Pierre Beauregard

Full Name: Pierre Gustave Toutant Beauregard
Born: May 28, 1818
Place of Birth: St. Bernard Parish, LA
North or South: South
Education: Graduate from West Pont in 1838.
Pre-War Profession: Mexican War, Superintendant of West Point in 1861, resigned February of 1861.
Post-War Profession: Railroad President, lottery supervisor, politician.
War Service Highlights: He commanded defenses south of Richmond, and spent time guarding the South Carolina coast. During Sherman's March through the state Beauregard was in charge of all the troops in South Carolina.
Nickname: None
Died: February 20, 1893
Place of Death: New Orleans, LA
Interesting Facts: He refused post-war offers to command foreign armies.

Judah Benjamin

Full Name: Judah P. Benjamin
Born: August 6, 1811
Place of Birth: St. Croix, Danish West Indies (Virgin Islands)
North or South: South
Education: None
Pre-War Profession: Commercial lawyer, political advocate for banking, Louisiana Legislature, taught at schools, studied law.
Post-War Profession: Publisher of Treatise on Law of Sale of Personal Property.
War Service Highlights: Benjamin served as Confederate secretary of war from 1861 to 1862 and a secretary of state from 1862 to 1865.
Nickname: None
Died: May 6, 1884
Place of Death: Paris, France
Interesting Facts: He was a U.S. senator, who some were convinced was the mastermind behind Lincolns assassination.

Braxton Bragg

Full Name: Braxton Bragg
Born: March 22, 1817
Place of Birth: Warrenton, North Carolina
North or South: South
Education: Graduated West Point, 1837
Pre-War Profession: Seminole War, Mexican War, Lieutenant Colonel, resigned 1856, planter.
Post-War Profession: Engineer
War Service Highlights: In 1861, Bragg served as a colonel and then major general in the Louisiana Militia. He commanded a corps under A.S. Johnston at Shiloh, and was promoted to full general. Bragg won the greatest Confederate victory in the Western Theater at the Battle of Chickamauga. He was removed from command shortly thereafter. He was made an advisor to Jefferson Davis.
Nickname: None
Died: September 27, 1876
Place of Death: Galveston, Texas
Interesting Facts: He had great patriotism and courage. He was a very devoted general who didn't praise others and he didn't allow himself to be praised either. He was a friend of President Davis.

John Breckenridge

Full Name: John Cabell Breckenridge
Born: January 15, 1821
Place of Birth: Lexington, Kentucky
North or South: South
Education: Centre College, Danville
Pre-War Profession: Lawyer, politician, US Congressman, US Vice President.
Post-War Profession: Exile in Cuba, returned to US, lawyer.
War Service Highlights: In October 1861, Breckenridge was a Brigadier General. He served mostly in the West. Breckenridge fought in battles at Vicksburg, Shiloh, Jackson and Chickamauga. From February to April, 1865, he served as secretary of war for the Confederacy. Breckinridge went to Europe when the South surrendered, and he returned in 1869.
Nickname: None
Died: May 17, 1875
Place of Death: Lexington, Kentucky
Interesting Facts: He was promoted to major at the beginning of the Mexican War. He became the Vice President of the United States.

Simon Bolivar Buckner

Full Name: Simon Bolivar Buckner
Born: April 1, 1823
Place of Birth: Hart City, Kentucky
North or South: South
Education: Graduated from West Point in 1844.
Pre-War Profession: Mexican War-resigned in 1855, businessman.
Post-War Profession: Editor of newspapers, Kentucky Governor, Vice-Presidential nominee 1896.
War Service Highlights: In 1861 he refused commission in the Union Army and he became a Brigadier General in the Confederate Army. In 1863 he commanded troops at the Battle of Chickamauga under the command of Braxton Bragg. He was also in command of the Department of East Tennessee. In 1864 he was promoted to Lieutenant General, and worked to have General Bragg removed from office.
Nickname: None
Died: January 8, 1914
Place of Death: Munfordville, Kentucky
Interesting Facts: Last survivor of the top three grades of the Confederate army.

Patrick Cleburne

Full Name: Patrick Ronayne Cleburne
Born: March 17, 1828
Place of Birth: County Cork, Ireland
North or South: South
Education: Unknown
Pre-War Profession: Served in 41st Regiment, British Army, emigrated to US, pharmacist, lawyer.
Post-War Profession: None
War Service Highlights: He was one of the greatest field commanders who came from Ireland in 1849. Cleburne served in several majors battles in the Civil War including the Battle of Shiloh, the Battle of Perryville, the Battle of Richmond and the Battle of Murfreesboro. He was wounded in the face at the Battle of Perryville. He earned the rank of major general following the Battle of Murfreesboro. Patrick Cleburne was nicknamed "Stonewall of the West" by Jefferson Davis. .
Nickname: None
Died: November 30, 1864
Place of Death: Franklin, Tennessee
Interesting Facts: He was great in combat. A general whose career was damaged by his proposal to muster slaves as combat soldiers.

Samuel Cooper

Full Name: Samuel Cooper
Born: June 12, 1798
Place of Birth: Hackensack, New Jersey
North or South: South
Education: Graduated from West Point, 1815.
Pre-War Profession: Seminole War, 1852, adjutant General.
Post-War Profession: Farmer
War Service Highlights: In March 1861, Cooper served as a Brigadier General in the Confederate Army.
Nickname: none
Died: December 3, 1876
Place of Death: Alexandria, Virginia
Interesting Facts: At the end of the war, he handed all records intact, to Federal authorities.

Jubal Early

Full Name: Jubal Anderson Early
Born: November 3, 1816
Place of Birth: Franklin City, Virginia
North or South: South
Education: West Point graduate of 1837.
Pre-War Profession: Seminole war lawyer, politician, Mexican War.
Post-War Profession: None
War Service Highlights: He commanded Early's Division/second Corps at Gettysburg.
Nickname: None
Died: March 2, 1894
Place of Death: Lynchburg, Virginia
Interesting Facts: Jubal never surrendered!

Richard Ewell

Full Name: Richard Stoddert Ewell
Born: February 8, 1817
Place of Birth: Georgetown, D.C.
North or South: South
Education: West Point Graduate, 1840.
Pre-War Profession: Ewell was in the Mexican War and he resigned in 1861.
Post-War Profession: He later became a farmer.
War Service Highlights: Ewell served in the Confederacy as a Lieutenant and then became a Colonel. He was promoted to Brigadier General in 1861. In 1862, he earned the rank of Major General. He served at First Bull Run, and then he fought through the seven day battles and at Cedar Mountain. Ewell fell off of his horse during the battle of Bloody Angle and he could not serve any longer.
Nickname: None
Died: January 25, 1872
Place of Death: Spring Hill, Tennessee
Interesting Facts: He was known for fighting until he had nothing left. He fought and rode his horse even when he had a wooden leg, but he fell off his horse making him even more disabled.

John Floyd

Full Name: John Buchanan Floyd
Born: June 1, 1806
Place of Birth: Montgomery City, Virginia
North or South: South
Education: Unknown
Pre-War Profession: Lawyer, cotton planter, politician, governor, Secretary of War to President Buchanan, resigned December 1860.
Post-War Profession: None
War Service Highlights: In May 1861, Floyd was a Brigadier General in the West Virginia campaign.
Died: August 26, 1863
Place of Death: Abingdon, Virginia
Interesting Facts: He was accused by the North of transferring material to Southern arsenals prior to the War.

Nathan Bedford Forrest

Full Name: Nathan Bedford Forrest
Born: July 13, 1821
Place of Birth: Bedford City, Tennessee
North or South: South
Education: Unknown
Pre-War Profession: Planter, slave dealer.
Post-War Profession: Planter, railroad president.
War Service Highlights: He commanded the cavalry in Hood's Franklin and Nashville campaign.
Nickname: None
Died: October 29, 1877
Place of Death: Memphis, Tennessee
Interesting Facts: The greatest cavalry leader of the war, associated with the Ku Klux Klan for a time after the war.

Wade Hampton

Full Name: Wade Hampton
Born: March 28, 1818
Place of Birth: Charleston, SC
North or South: South
Education: Unknown
Pre-War Profession: Politician, farmer/planter.
Post-War Profession: He became a planter, a governor and a United States Senator.
War Service Highlights: Hampton was a commander during the Civil War for the Army of the North Virginia Calvary Corps. Hampton was in charge of the Hampton Legion and fought at First Manassas. He was also involved in the battles at Peninsula, Antietam, and Gettysburg. He was made a Major General in 1864.
Nickname: None
Died: April 11, 1902
Place of Death: Columbia, South Carolina
Interesting Facts: Hampton was one of three Confederate generals that did not have proper military training.

William Hardee

Full Name: William Joseph Hardee
Born: October 12, 1815
Place of Birth: Camden City, Georgia
North or South: South
Education: West Point graduate of 1838.
Pre-War Profession: Hardee was involved in the Mexican War, he was put in command of cadets at West Point, wrote a textbook on tactics, he resigned in January, 1861.
Post-War Profession: After the Civil War, Hardee became a planter.
War Service Highlights: Hardee first served as a Colonel and then a Brigadier General in the Confederacy in 1861. He became a Major General in October of 1861 and fought at the Battle of Shiloh. He also commanded the Department of South Carolina, Georgia, and Florida but surrendered these divisions on April 26, 1865.
Nickname: "Old Reliable"
Died: November 6, 1873
Place of Death: Wytheville, Virginia
Interesting Facts: He was an outstanding Corps commander.

Ambrose Powell Hill

Full Name: Ambrose Powell Hill
Born: November 9, 1825
Place of Birth: Culpepper, Virginia
North or South: South
Education: West Point Graduate of 1847.
Pre-War Profession: Mexican War, Seminole war, resigned March 1861.
Post-War Profession: None
War Service Highlights: A.P. Hill was a colonel in the 13th Virginia Infantry, and served in the battle of First Bull Run. He was made a brigadier general and commanded troops in the Army of the Potomac. A.P. Hill was one of the most successful commanders of Robert E. Lee's Army of Northern Virginia serving as a Major General. A.P. Hill troops were known as the Light Division. His troops fought in the Seven Days Battles, Cedar Mountain, Second Bull Run, Antietam, and Fredericksburg. He was promoted to Lieutenant General in 1863.
Nickname: None
Died: April 2, 1865
Place of Death: Petersburg, Virginia
Interesting Facts: Although he was a famous fighter, his performance was not good after being given a Corps command.

Daniel Hill

Full Name: Daniel Harvey Hill
Born: July 12, 1821
Place of Birth: York District, South Carolina
North or South: South
Education: Graduated from West Point in 1842
Pre-War Profession: He was in the Mexican War, and he resigned in 1849. He was a college professor, and a superintendent of North Carolina Military Institute.
Post-War Profession: He was and editor, and a college president.
War Service Highlights: Daniel Hill became a Brigadier General after winning the Battle of Big Bethel. In 1862, He fought at the Battle of Yorktown, Williamsburg, and Seven Pines and was promoted to Major General. He served at the Seven Days Battle, and the Battles of Second Bull Run, South Mountain, and Antietam under General Robert E. Lee.
Nickname: None
Died: September 24, 1889
Place of Death: Charlotte North Carolina
Interesting Facts: 15 members of his West Point class became Civil war generals. He was brave but abrasive, and could have been used much more effectively for the Confederate cause.

John Bell Hood

Full Name: John Bell Hood
Born: June 1, 1831
Place of Birth: Owensville, Kentucky
North or South: South
Education: Graduate of West Point in 1853.
Pre-War Profession: Frontier duty with 2nd Cavalry, resigned April 1861.
Post-War Profession: Unsuccessful businessman, wrote memoirs, died of yellow fever.
War Service Highlights: John Hood was commander of the Texas Brigade. In August, 1862, he commanded troops at the Second Battle of Bull Run and in September of that same year he fought in the battle of Antietam. He fought as a General at Fredericksburg and was then wounded while fighting at Gettysburg in 1863. In the battle at Chickamauga, in 1863, he lost his right leg. He was promoted to General and became commander of the Army of Tennessee. While in command, he lost every battle.
Nickname: None
Died: August 30, 1879
Place of Death: New Orleans, LA
Interesting Facts: He was a rash fighter. He performed well in subordinate roles, not as an army commander.

Stonewall Jackson

Full Name: Thomas Jonathan Jackson
Born: January 21, 1824
Place of Birth: Clarksburg, Virginia
North or South: South
Education: West Point graduate of 1846.
Pre-War Profession: Mexican War, 1851 resigned from US army, professor at VMI.
Post-War Profession: None
War Service Highlights: Thomas J. Jackson, also known as Stonewall Jackson, was a Confederate commander. It was at the Battle of Manassas that he was given the nickname Stonewall. In 1861, he was a Major in the Virginia militia and Colonel of the Confederate infantry at Harper's Ferry. In October of 1862, he was promoted to Lieutenant General and commanded the new second Corps. He was in charge of half of the Army of Northern Virginia. Port Republic, Front Royal, and Cross Keys were also victories that Jackson celebrated as the most revered of Confederate commanders.
Nickname: "Stonewall"
Died: May 10, 1863
Place of Death: Guiney's Station, Virginia
Interesting Facts: Jackson is known as one of the greatest commanders of the south.

Albert Sidney Johnston

Full Name: Albert Sidney Johnston
Born: February 2, 1803
Place of Birth: Washington, Kentucky
North or South: South
Education: Graduated West Point, 1826
Pre-War Profession: Black Hawk war, Mexican War, fought for Texas independence, Colonel of US 2nd Cavalry, Utah expedition, commanded Department of the Pacific, resigned April 1861.
Post-War Profession: None
War Service Highlights: Johnston was in command of the Confederate Department Number Two.
Nickname: None
Died: April 6, 1862
Place of Death: Pittsburg Landing, Tennessee
Interesting Facts: A close friend of President Davis. It's thought that as a result of an old injury, he had loss of feeling in his leg and this contributed to his bleeding to death at Shiloh.

Joseph Johnston

Full Name: Joseph Eggleston Johnston
Born: February 3, 1807
Place of Birth: Farmville, Virginia
North or South: South
Education: He was a West Point Graduate of 1829.
Pre-War Profession: Frontier Duty, he resigned from this in 1837, civil engineer, commissioned in US army in 1838, Mexican War, June 1860 Brigadier General, resigned in April of 1861.
Post-War Profession: He later became a U.S. Congressman, commissioner of railroads, wrote memoirs.
War Service Highlights: He commanded the Army of Tennessee.
Nickname: None
Died: March 21, 1819
Place of Death: Washington, D.C.
Interesting Facts: He served in the Black Hawk and Seminole wars. He left the army in 1837 to become a civil engineer, but a year after that he was reappointed as an army lieutenant.

Fitzhugh Lee

Full Name: Fitzhugh Lee
Born: November 19, 1835
Place of Birth: Fairfax City, Virginia
North or South: South
Education: West Point Graduate of 1856.
Pre-War Profession: Frontier duty, instructor at West Point, resigned May 1861.
Post-War Profession: Farmer, governor, consul general at Havana, Maj. Gen. of US Volunteers in Spanish-American war.
War Service Highlights: Lee became a first lieutenant in the Confederate Army in 1861 following in his uncle Robert E. Lee's footsteps. Between 1861 and 1863 he was promoted to lieutenant colonel, brigadier general and then to Major General. His greatest achievement while serving in the war was at the Battle of Chancellorsville.
Nickname: None
Died: April 28, 1905
Place of Death: Washington, D.C.
Interesting Facts: Fitzhugh was the nephew of Robert E. Lee and General Samuel Cooper.

Robert E. Lee

Full Name: Robert Edward Lee
Born: January 19, 1807
Place of Birth: Westmoreland City, Virginia
North or South: South
Education: Graduated West Point, 1829
Pre-War Profession: Engineering duty, Mexican War, superintendent of West Point, 2nd Cavalry, commanded the forces that captured John Brown's body of men at Harper's Ferry, refused the offer of command of US forces at the outbreak of the War, resigned April 1861.
Post-War Profession: President of Washington (later Washington and Lee) College.
War Service Highlights: He commanded the Army of Northern Virginia until the surrender at Appomattox.
Nickname: None
Died: October 12, 1870
Place of Death: Lexington, Virginia
Interesting Facts: He was known as the greatest of the Southern generals. Robert E. Lee was an idol to the Southerners. Lee always was ready to take the risks he had to. He was always energetic to attack or defend, whatever the challenge was.

Stephen Lee

Full Name: Stephen Dill Lee
Born: September 22, 1833
Place of Birth: Charleston, South Carolina
North or South: South
Education: Graduated at West Point, 1854.
Pre-War Profession: Artillery and staff duty, resigned February 1861.
Post-War Profession: Farmer, politician, college president.
War Service Highlights: He took over command of Hood's Corps in Army of Tennessee.
Nickname: None
Died: May 28, 1908
Place of Death: Vicksburg, Mississippi
Interesting Facts: Youngest Confederate Lieutenant Gen. A distant relative of R. E. Lee.

James Longstreet

Full Name: James Longstreet
Born: January 8, 1821
Place of Birth: Edgefield District, South Carolina
North or South: South
Education: He graduated from West Point in 1842.
Pre-War Profession: He was in Indian campaigns, the Mexican War, and resigned in June, 1861.
Post-War Profession: He was an Insurance agent, a lottery supervisor, a US minister to Turkey, and he wrote memoirs.
War Service Highlights: He was in command of I Corps of Army of Northern Virginia.
Nickname: "Old Pete"
Died: January 2, 1904
Place of Death: Gainesville, Georgia
Interesting Facts: At age 12, his father died and his family moved to Somerville, Alabama. He became a close advisor to R. E. Lee. Criticized by many former Confederates and then he got back with his book, *From Manassas to Appomattox.* He also had a talent for defensive fighting and he showed it.

William Mahone

Full Name: William Mahone
Born: December 1, 1826
Place of Birth: Monroe, Virginia
North or South: South
Education: Unknown.
Pre-War Profession: Teacher at the Rappahannock Academy, Superintendent of the Norfolk and Petersburg railroad.
Post-War Profession: Returned to engineering and continued to be instrumental in developing railway system in Virginia.
War Service Highlights: William Mahone served as a Lieutenant Colonel and a Brigadier General. He led his troops at Seven Pines and at Malvern Hill. He also fought at 2nd Manassas, Fredericksburg, Chancellorsville, Gettysburg, the Wilderness, and Spotsylvania. William Mahone was made a Major General in 1864 for his service at the Battle of the Crater.
Nickname: None
Died: October 8, 1895
Place of Death: Petersburg, Virginia
Interesting Facts: Mahone worked as a mail boy before becoming a railroad superintendent.

John Mosby

Full Name: John Singleton Mosby
Born: December 6, 1833
Place of Birth: Edgemont, Virginia
North or South: Mosby was a southern general.
Education: University of Virginia, 1849
Pre-War Profession: Mosby was a Lawyer in Bristol before the war.
Post-War Profession: Unknown
War Service Highlights: John Mosby was a private in the first Virginia Calvary in 1861 and then served as a first lieutenant in 1862. He served as a major in the 43rd Virginia Calvary Battalion in 1863 and as a Lieutenant Colonel in the 43rd Virginia Calvary Battalion in 1864. He was also appointed a Colonel in the Virginia Cavalry Regiment in December of 1864.
Nickname: None
Died: 1916
Place of Death: Unknown
Interesting Facts: He captured Brigadier General Stoughton.

William Dorsey Pender

Full Name: William Dorsey Pender
Born: February 6, 1834
Place of Birth: Edgecombe City, North Carolina
North or South: South
Education: Graduated from West Point, 1854.
Pre-War Profession: Clerk, duty on the Pacific coast, resigned March 1861.
Post-War Profession: None
War Service Highlights: He commanded Pender's Division/third Corps. Pender began his service in the war as a Captain and then he was promoted to Colonel and then Brigadier General in 1862. He was later made a Major General in May of 1863. He fought during the Seven Days Battles, Second Bull Run, Antietam, Fredericksburg and Chancellorsville. Pender
Nickname: None
Died: July 18, 1863
Place of Death: Staunton, Virginia
Interesting Facts: He was one of the best fighters in the Army of Northern Virginia. He was the youngest General killed at Gettysburg at age 29.

George Pickett

Full Name: George Edward Pickett
Born: January 28, 1825
Place of Birth: Richmond, Virginia
North or South: South
Education: Graduated from West Point in 1846.
Pre-War Profession: He was in the Mexican War and had frontier duty. He went against the British at San Juan Island and resigned in 1861.
Post-War Profession: Insurance Agent
War Service Highlights: He commanded the Departments of Virginia and North Carolina.
Nickname: None
Died: July 30, 1875
Place of Death: Norfolk, Virginia
Interesting Facts: He was a colonel, then a brigadier general who served under Major General Longstreet.

Leonidas Polk

Full Name: Leonidas Polk
Born: April 10, 1806
Place of Birth: Raleigh, North Carolina
North or South: South
Education: Graduated from West Point in 1827.
Pre-War Profession: Minister, bishop.
Post-War Profession: None
War Service Highlights: Polk entered the war as a Major General. He fought at the Battles of Shiloh, Corinth, Murfreesboro, and Chickamauga in 1863. He commanded Polk's Corps in the Atlanta campaign.
Nickname: None
Died: June 14, 1864
Place of Death: Pine Mountain, Georgia
Interesting Facts: A favorite of President Davis. He didn't cost the Confederate any battle.

William Quantrill

Full Name: William Quantrill
Born: July 31, 1837
Place of Birth: Ohio
North or South: South
Education: Unknown
Pre-War Profession: Teacher, professional.
Post-War Profession: Went around raiding, murdering, etc. He lead Quantrill's Raiders.
War Service: Not officially affiliated with the Southern forces.
Nickname: None
Died: June 6, 1865
Place of Death: Unknown
Interesting Facts: He also gained a reputation for murdering members of the Union Army that the gang had taken prisoner. He killed 150 people and destroyed 180 buildings in one raid.

Robert Rodes

Full Name: Robert Emmet Rodes
Born: March 29, 1829
Place of Birth: Lynchburg, Virginia
North or South: South
Education: Graduated from VMI in 1848.
Pre-War Profession: Assistant professor, civil engineer.
Post-War Profession: None
War Service Highlights: Rodes became a Brigadier General in October of 1861 and he commanded a division at Chancellorsville. He was wounded at Seven Pines and at Sharpsburg. He was promoted to Major General by Stonewall Jackson.
Nickname: None
Died: September 19, 1864
Place of Death: Winchester, Virginia
Interesting Facts: A modest, but inspiring leader.

JEB Stuart

Full Name: James Ewell Brown Stuart
Born: February 6, 1833
Place of Birth: Patrick City, Virginia
North or South: South
Education: Graduated at West Point in 1854.
Pre-War Profession: Served in first cavalry on frontier duty, aide to R. E. Lee when John Brown's body of men fought at Harper's Ferry, May 1861, resigned U.S. army.
Post-War Profession: None
War Service Highlights: He was in command of all the cavalry in the Army of Northern Virginia. He also served as a Colonel and a Brigadier General in the 1st Virginia Cavalry in 1861 and as a Major General in 1862.
Nickname: "Jeb"
Died: May 12, 1864
Place of Death: Richmond, Virginia
Interesting Facts: Criticized for straying too far from Lee in the march to Gettysburg, he, thereafter, kept in close communication with the Army of Northern Virginia.

Stand Watie

Full Name: Stand Watie
Born: December 12, 1806
Place of Birth: Rome, Georgia
North or South: South
Education: Unknown
Pre-War Profession: Planter, newspaper publisher, signed a treaty, which gave up Cherokee lands in Georgia, to move to Oklahoma.
Post-War Profession: Planter, businessman.
War Service Highlights: In May 1864, Watie was a Brigadier General who captured the steamer J. R. Williams.
Nickname: None
Died: September 9, 1871
Place of Death: Delaware City, Oklahoma
Interesting Facts: The last Confederate general to surrender his command.

Joseph Wheeler

Full Name: Joseph Wheeler
Born: September 10, 1836
Place of Birth: Augusta, Georgia
North or South: South
Education: West Point Graduate of 1859
Pre-War Profession: Frontier duty, resigned from frontier duty on April 1861.
Post-War Profession: Cotton planter, United states congressman, in the Spanish-American war he was a Major General of volunteers, commander in the Philippines, commissioned a Brig. General in the Regular Army.
War Service Highlights: He was in the Atlanta campaign, and he commanded the Cavalry Corps. He was also was opposed to Sherman's March to the Sea.
Nickname: "Fightin' Joe"
Died: January 25, 1906
Place of Death: Brooklyn, NY
Interesting Facts: Second only to Nathan Forrest as a raider. He was a General for both the North and the South.

Famous Women of the Civil War

Princess Agnes

Full Name: Princess Agnes Leclerc Salm-Salm
Born: December 25, 1844
Place of Birth: Franklin, Vermont
North or South: North
Died: December 21, 1912
Place of Death: Unknown
Interesting Facts: She acted as a nurse/doctor, stole supplies meant for the officers, and used them for the wounded.

Louisa May Alcott

Full Name: Louisa May Alcott
Born: November 29, 1832
Place of Birth: Germantown, Pennsylvania
North or South: North
Died: March 6, 1888
Place of Death: Concord, Massachusetts
Interesting Facts: She was a nurse during the Civil War. She was an American Novelist best known for her novel *Little Women,* published in 1868. She published over 30 books, and collections of stories. She began to work at an early age.

Susan B. Anthony

Full Name: Susan Brownell Anthony
Born: February 15, 1820
Place of Birth: Adams, Massachusetts
North or South: North
Died: March 13, 1906
Place of Death: Rochester, New York
Interesting Facts: She went to her father's school, and then to a Boarding School in Philadelphia. She aided the administration of President Abraham Lincoln, and aided wounded soldiers during the war. She did all this before fighting for the right of women to vote.

Clara Barton

Full Name: Clarissa Harlowe Barton
Born: December 25, 1821
Place of Birth: Oxford, Massachusetts
North or South: North
Died: 1912
Place of Death: Washington, D.C.
Interesting Facts: Clara delivered aid to soldiers of the North and South. In 1881 she established the American Red Cross and served as the director until her death. She also established a free school in Bordentown, New Jersey before the American Civil War.

Mary Bickerdyke

Full Name: Mary Bickerdyke
Born: July 19, 1817
Place of Birth: Know County, Ohio
North or South: North
Died: November 8, 1901
Place of Death: Bunker Hill, Kansas
Interesting Facts: "Mother Bickerdyke" joined a field hospital at Fort Donelson. She worked on the first hospital boat, collecting wounded soldiers from Cairo, Louisville and St. Louis. She eventually became chief of nursing for Ulysses S. Grant.

Mary Elizabeth Bowser

Full Name: Mary Elizabeth Bowser
Born: 1840's
Place of Birth: On a plantation near Richmond, Virginia
North or South: South
Died: 1900
Place of Death: Unknown
Interesting Facts: Mary served as a spy for Ulysses S. Grant.

Belle Boyd

Full Name: Maria Isabella Boyd
Born: May 4, 1844
Place of Birth: Martinsburg, Virginia
North or South: South
Died: 1900
Place of Death: Kilbourne City, Wisconsin.
Interesting Facts: She was one of the most famous Confederate Spies. Generals Turner, Ashby and Stonewall Jackson made her a captain and honorary aide-de-camp on his staff. She was arrested by the U.S. Secret Service.

Harriet Jacobs

Full Name: Linda Brent (Harriet A. Jacobs)
Born: 1813
Place of Birth: North Carolina
North or South: North
Died: 1897
Place of Death: Washington, D.C.
Interesting Facts: Harriet was six years old before she realized she was a slave. Her mother died and she went to live with her mistress. When her mistress died, she went to live with her master named Jacobs. She escaped and hid in her grandmother's attic for seven years. Then, she was hidden on a boat and taken to the north for freedom. To protect her grandmother, children, and other living relatives, she published her memoirs under the name of Linda Brent.

Kady Brownell

Full Name: Kady Brownell
Born: 1842
Place of Birth: In an army camp in Caffaria, on the African Coast
North or South: North
Died: Unknown
Place of Death: Unknown
Interesting Facts: She signed up to be in the Rhode Island Infantry for three months.

Anna Carroll

Full Name: Anna Ella Carroll
Born: 1815
Place of Birth: Maryland's Eastern Shore
North or South: North
Died: 1894
Place of Death: Washington, D.C.
Interesting Facts: She was a strategist, whose reports resulted in major military strategies.

Mary Chesnutt

Full Name: Mary Boykin Miller Chesnutt
Born: March 31, 1823
Place of Birth: Statesboro, South Carolina
North or South: South
Died: November 22, 1886
Place of Death: Camden, South Carolina
Interesting Facts: She wrote famous diaries about the Civil War, which were later published.

Pauline Cushman

Full Name: Pauline Cushman
Born: 1833
Place of Birth: New Orleans, Louisiana
North or South: North
Died: 1893
Place of Death: She was buried with the military in San Francisco, California.
Interesting Facts: She was a Union spy. She was an actress, then a Civil War spy who was ultimately captured and sentenced to be executed by the South. She was rescued three days before her death, and she was given the honorary commission of Major by President Abraham Lincoln.

Varina Davis

Full Name: Varina Howell Davis
Born: May 7, 1826
Place of Birth: Natchez, Mississippi
North or South: South
Died: October 16, 1905
Place of Death: New York
Interesting Facts: As the wife of Jefferson Davis, she was the First Lady of the confederacy.

Sarah Morgan Dawson

Full Name: Sarah Morgan Dawson
Born: 1842
Place of Birth: New Orleans, Louisiana
North or South: North
Died: 1909
Place of Death: Paris, France
Interesting Facts: She wrote a diary about the Civil War, starting when she was 20 years old.

Dorothea Dix

Full Name: Dorothea Lynde Dix
Born: April 4, 1802
Place of Birth: Hampden, Maine
North or South: North
Died: July 17, 1887
Place of Death: A hospital in Trenton, New Jersey that she had founded.
Interesting Facts: She taught in many different schools. She inspired legislators in 15 U.S. states and Canada to establish hospitals for the mentally ill. In 1861 she was appointed superintendant of army nurses for the Civil War service.

Sarah Edmonds

Full Name: Sarah Emma Edmonds
Born: December, 1841
Place of Birth: Brunswick, Canada
North or South: North
Died: September 5, 1898
Place of Death: La Porte, Texas
Interesting Facts: She was one of 400 women who enlisted in the army during the Civil War. She was successful as a Union spy while impersonating a man.

Anna Ethridge

Full Name: Anna Ethridge
Born: May 3, 1844
Place of Birth: Detroit, Michigan
North or South: North
Died: Unknown
Place of Death: Unknown
Interesting Facts: She helped the wounded at Blackburn's Ford as well as both battles at Bull Run.

Antonia Ford

Full Name: Antonia Ford
Born: 1838
Place of Birth: Fairfax, Virginia
North or South: South
Died: 1871
Place of Death: Fairfax, Virginia
Interesting Facts: She saved many Southern troops.

Barbara Frietchie

Full Name: Barbara Frietchie
Born: December 3, 1766
Place of Birth: Lancaster, Pennsylvania
North or South: North
Died: December 18, 1862
Place of Death: Frederick, Maryland
Interesting Facts: At 95 years old she stuck the Union flag out of her window as the Confederate troops were riding by. When Stonewall Jackson rode by he ordered his troops to shoot the flag. After he ordered them to shoot she said to him, "Shoot if you must, but spare your country's flag." Her bravery and patriotism inspired John Greenleaf Whittier to write the poem Barbara Fritchie, published in 1863.

Julia Grant

Full Name: Julia Dent Grant
Born: January 26, 1826
Place of Birth: St. Louis, Missouri
North or South: North
Died: December 14, 1902
Place of Death: New York City
Interesting Facts: Julia Dent was the wife of General and future President Ulysses S. Grant. She was captured by Southern troops, but released when her identity was revealed.

Rose O'Neal Greenhow

Full Name: Rose O'Neal Greenhow
Born: 1817
Place of Birth: Montgomery County, Maryland
North or South: North
Died: October, 1864
Place of Death: Buried in Oakdale Cemetery, Maryland
Interesting Facts: She was a spy. She sent a secret message to General Pierre G.T. Beauregard which caused him to win the battle of Bull Run. She developed a close association with Lieutenant Colonel Thomas Jordan of Virginia, a former quartermaster in the United States Army who was in the process of developing a Confederate spy network in the federal Capital. From Jordan, Greenhow learned how to use a 26-symbol cipher, and began her connections with the prominent Unionists for the purpose of eliciting information that she then transmitted in code to relevant figures in the Confederacy.

Nancy Hart

Full Name: Nancy Morgan Hart
Born: 1846
Place of Birth: Raleigh, North Carolina
North or South: South
Died: 1913
Place of Death: Mannings Knob, West Virginia
Interesting Facts: William Price, Nancy's stepbrother, never got to Spencer to make a speech, he was found three days later, shot in the back near another farm on the road to Spencer. Nancy began to hate the Union troops. Nancy's next door neighbor's the Kelly's had two son's join the Confederate Army. The Kelly's threw a going away party, which Nancy went to. While the party was going on, Union Soldiers marched past the house. The music stopped, she threw her hands over her head and shouted "HURRAH FOR JEFF DAVIS" . Four rifles fired and four minie balls struck the front stoop, one of then lodged in the door facing Nancy. Three nights later she saddled up and rode away and her career as a Confederate Spy began.

Cordelia Harvey

Full Name: Cordelia Adelaide Perrine Harvey
Born: 1824
Place of Birth: Kenosha, Wisconsin
North or South: North
Died: 1895
Place of Death: Buffalo, New York
Interesting Facts: Known as "The Wisconsin Angel," she helped start Veterans hospitals. After her husband died, she was appointed to the Sanitary Commission and started to work in Union hospitals.

Esther Hawks

Full Name: Dr. Esther Hill Hawks
Born: 1833
Place of Birth: Unknown
North or South: North
Died: 1906
Place of Death: Unknown
Interesting Facts: She went to medical school. Dorothea Dix rejected her application for duty as a nurse because she was too young and pretty. She went to the South to teach slaves to read and write. Eventually she opened a hospital in Boston.

Lucy Hayes

Full Name: Lucy Webb Hayes
Born: 1831
Place of Birth: Fremont, Ohio
North or South: North
Died: 1889
Place of Death: Fremont, Ohio
Interesting Facts: She went to the camp that her husband was stationed at and ministered the wounded, cheered the homesick, and comforted the dying. She later became the First Lady of the United States when her husband, Rutherford B. Hayes, was elected President.

Abbey House

Full Name: Abbey House
Born: 1797
Place of Birth: Franklin, North Carolina
North or South: South
Died: 1881
Place of Death: Raleigh, North Carolina
Interesting Facts: On her gravestone "Angel Of Mercy To Confederate Soldiers" was written. She was also the first woman ever to vote.

Julia Ward Howe

Full Name: Julia Ward Howe
Born: May 27, 1819
Place of Birth: New York, New York
North or South: North
Died: October 17, 1910
Place of Death: Boston, Massachusetts
Interesting Facts: Today she is best known as the writer of the *Battle Hymn of the Republic.* She became active in women's rights later in her life.

Madame La Force

Full Name: Madame La Force
Born: NA
Place of Birth: NA
North or South: South
Died: NA
Place of Death: NA
Interesting Facts: Madame LaForce was not a real woman, but a man dressed as a woman in order to spy on the enemy.

Mary Custis Lee

Full Name: Mary Anne Randolph Custis Lee
Born: October 1, 1808
Place of Birth: Arlington, Virginia
North or South: South
Died: November 5, 1873
Place of Death: Lexington, Virginia
Interesting Facts: Mary Custis was the wife of Confederate General Robert E. Lee.

Mary Todd Lincoln

Full Name: Mary Todd Lincoln
Born: December 13, 1818
Place of Birth: Lexington, Kentucky
North or South: North
Died: July 16, 1882
Place of Death: Springfield, Illinois
Interesting Facts: Mary's family was from the South. Her family owned slaves and her brothers fought for the Confederacy. She met Abraham Lincoln and they fell in love. Soon they got engaged, but Abraham asked Mary to release the engagement. After a period of time, Mary's friend arranged for them to be engaged again. Mary Todd Lincoln was the mother of four children, only one of whom lived to be an adult. She was present at the assassination of her husband and had a mental breakdown after the incident.

Ella Palmer

Full Name: Ella Palmer
Born: 1829
Place of Birth: Tennessee
North or South: South
Died: November 7, 1909
Place of Death: Lake City, Colorado
Interesting Facts: Ella was asked to help save wounded Confederate soldiers. She and her daughter went to a hospital and found wounded soldiers lying on the floor. Not only did she help save the Confederate soldiers she also took charge as the head matron of the hospital.

Phoebe Pember

Full Name: Phoebe Yates Levy Pember
Born: August 18, 1823
Place of Birth: Charleston, South Carolina
North or South: South
Died: 1913
Place of Death: Pittsburg, Pennsylvania
Interesting Facts: She received an offer to serve as a matron of the Chimborazo Military Hospital, from Mrs. George W. Randolph, the wife of the Confederate Secretary of War.

Emma Sansom

Full Name: Emma Sansom
Born: 1846
Place of Birth: Gadsden, Alabama
North or South: South
Died: 1900
Place of Death: Gadsden, Alabama
Interesting Facts: She led General Forest's men across Black Creek to capture enemy troops.

Sarah Thompson

Full Name: Sarah Elizabeth Thompson
Born: February 11, 1838
Place of Birth: Greene County, Tennessee
North or South: South
Died: 1909
Place of Death: Washington, D.C.
Interesting Facts: She worked alongside her husband, Sylvanuis H. Thompson, a recruiter for the Union Army.

Sally Tompkins

Full Name: Sally Tompkins
Born: November 9, 1833
Place of Birth: Matthews County, Virginia
North or South: South
Died: 1916
Place of Death: Richmond, Virginia
Interesting Facts: She established her own private hospital. Even though most hospitals had to close because they couldn't get medical supplies from the government, because her hospital had the highest recovery rate, Confederate President Jefferson Davis, let her keep it open.

Harriet Tubman

Full Name: Harriet Tubman
Born: 1820
Place of Birth: Dorchester County, Maryland
North or South: North
Died: March 10, 1913
Place of Death: Auburn, New York
Interesting Facts: During the Civil War she was a nurse, scout, and spy for the Union army in South Carolina and Florida. She was a runaway slave, and an underground railroad conductor, who led more than 300 slaves to freedom.

Mary Walker

Full Name: Dr. Mary Edwards Walker
Born: November 26, 1832
Place of Birth: Oswego, New York
North or South: North
Died: 1919
Place of Death: Oswego, New York
Interesting Facts: She was the only woman to receive the Congressional Medal of Honor for her service during the Civil War. Her birthplace on the Bunker Hill Road is marked with a historical marker.

Famous Units of the Civil War

Certain fighting groups on both sides distinguished themselves from others during the various conflicts. The 20th Maine became famous at Gettysburg, the 54th Massachusetts at Fort Wagner and certainly, the Irish Brigade and the Zouave units for many battles during the war.

The 20th Maine

The 20th Maine began its existence on August 20, 1862, with Adelbert Ames as its commander. It became most famous during the Battle of Gettysburg, when the unit repelled Confederate troops on Little Round Top. At that time, it was commanded by Colonel Joshua Chamberlain. Chamberlain left the unit later in 1863, when he was promoted to General.

* * * *

The 54th Massachusetts

The 54th Massachusetts was created in March, 1863 by Robert Gould Shaw. As one of the first black units utilized, its performance would be considered an important indication of the possibilities surrounding the use of African Americans in combat. Among the recruits were two sons of famous abolitionist, Frederick Douglass. The black soldiers proved themselves in battle many times, but were still paid less than white soldiers. The first black soldier to receive the Congressional Medal of Honor was William Carney.

The Irish Brigade

The Irish Brigade was actually created before the Civil War. It was created using Irish immigrants from New York, Pennsylvania and Massachusetts by Thomas Francis Meagher. Their nickname was the 'Sons of Erin' and their motto was 'Faugh A Ballaugh' or 'Clear the Way'. The Irish Brigade were known as fearless fighters and lost many men during the war. In fact, by 1863, they had lost 2,700 of 3,000 men. They lost another 300 out of 600 during the Battle of Gettysburg.

The Pennsylvania Bucktails

The 13th Pennsylvania Reserves were created in 1861 using lumbermen from the mountains of northern Pennsylvania. They had an unusual 'wildcat yell' and were known for their wild ways and disorderly conduct. They became known as the 'Bucktails' because of their tradition of wearing deer tails on their hats. They were superior marksmen and skirmishers. Some of these men served as President Lincoln's bodyguards until his assassination.

* * * *

Berdan's Sharpshooters

Hiram Berdan, the top rifle shot in the country at the time, was commissioned a Colonel in command of the 1st Regiment of U.S. Sharpshooters on November 30, 1861. He recruited the best marksmen from all over the country to serve as snipers. Every recruit had to be able to shoot ten bullets into a five inch target from 200 yards away. Each man received a Sharps target rifle and a forest green uniform for camouflage purposes. There were 2,570 sharpshooters during the war, 1,008 of whom were killed.

* * * *

Corcoran Legion

The 'Corcoran Legion' was made up of four New York regiments recruited by General Michael Corcoran. This group was made up of mostly Irish immigrants. In the beginning, the group was assigned to the Washington, D.C. area and saw no action. In late 1863, Corcoran was killed in a riding accident and was replaced by General Robert Tyler. In 1864, the unit was part of Grant's drive to Richmond and took a large number of casualties. During the Battle of Cold Harbor, almost the entire group was destroyed.

The 1st Delaware

The 1st Delaware first saw action at the Battle of Antietam, where almost 300 of its 650 men were killed. The unit was almost completely wiped out during the Battle of Fredericksburg during a suicidal charge. During the Battle of Gettysburg, they helped to stop Pickett's Charge Its commander, General Thomas Smyth was the last Northern General to be killed in the war.

* * * *

The 23rd Ohio

The 23rd Ohio is best known for being the unit which contained future Presidents of the United States, Rutherford B. Hayes and William McKinley.

* * * *

The IX Corps

The IX Corps was created on July 22, 1862 and commanded by General Ambrose Burnside. It has the distinction of having travelled further (seven states) and having lost more of its high ranking officers than any other Northern unit.

* * * *

The 2nd Wisconsin (The Iron Brigade)

The Iron Brigade was made up of soldiers from Wisconsin. They were nicknamed the Iron Brigade, because they 'stood like iron' in the face of their enemies. This unit lost 80 percent of its men at Gettysburg.

The 1st Minnesota

The 1st Minnesota is known for its charge at the Battle of Gettysburg. The men crossed over 200 yards of open ground and charged the Southerners in spite of the dire situation. Almost 200 of the 300 men were killed or wounded, but managed to hold off the Confederates.

* * * *

The Army of the Tennessee

The Army of the Tennessee was created using mostly western soldiers on October 16, 1862. Its first commander was General Ulysses S. Grant, then General William T. Sherman, General James B. McPherson and finally General Oliver O. Howard. They saw almost no fighting with Confederate troops, but waged total war on the Southern civilian population. This army had the best combat record of the war, never losing a major battle.

* * * *

Zouave

Colonel Elmer Ellsworth brought the concept or Zouave Troops to the United States, from Europe. They were known for their colorful uniforms and fierce fighting style. Ellsworth was the first person killed in the war, but almost 250 other Zouave units were formed on both sides. One of the most famous Zouave units was the 5th New York, led by Colonel Hiram Duryea.

The Orphan Brigade

The 1st Kentucky Brigade was created in 1861 as a Confederate unit. As Kentucky remained in the Union, the soldiers were forced to leave Kentucky, creating the nickname 'The Orphan Brigade.' President Lincoln's brother-in-law, Ben H. Helm was one of the brigade's generals. Former U.S. Vice President John C. Breckinridge was one of its division commanders. They were known as some of the best fighters in the Southern Army. By the end of the war, 3,500 of 4,000 men had been lost.

* * * *

The 26th North Carolina

Created on August 27, 1861, the 26th North Carolina spent the first year of the war in North Carolina doing nothing. In 1862, they became part of General Lee's Army of Northern Virginia and fought at Gettysburg in 1863. 600 of 800 men were killed on the first day at Gettysburg and only 90 survived Pickett's Charge. Almost 1,900 of 2,000 men were killed by the end of the war, an astounding 88 percent loss.

* * * *

The 6th Louisiana Tigers

The other name for the Tigers was 'The Wharf Rats' as most of the men came from the docks of New Orleans. They were famous for their colorful uniforms, fearlessness, hard fighting, drunkenness, thievery and desertion. In fact, almost 20 percent of the men left as deserters. They were disbanded in 1863.

Gregg's Brigade

This Confederate brigade was formed in 1862, serving alongside A.P. Hill and Stonewall Jackson. They lost almost 1,000 of 2,500 men in the Seven Days' Battles and lost 600 men during the Second Battle of Bull Run. General Maxcy Gregg and his men ran out of ammunition that day and they were forced to hold their position in hand to hand combat. Gregg's Brigade saved Lee's army at Harper's Ferry, but Gregg himself was killed at the Battle of Fredericksburg.

* * * *

Washington Artillery

Created in 1838, during the Mexican War, the Washington Artillery joined the Confederate Army in 1861. It was made up of mostly wealthy and prominent men from New Orleans. After the First Battle of Manassas, they joined the Army of Northern Virginia with Robert E. Lee and distinguished itself at Fredericksburg and Chancellorsville.

* * * *

The 9th Virginia

The 9th Virginia was also known as Armistead's Brigade. It was created on June 3, 1861. The reputation of the group was damaged after a retreat during the Battle of Seven Pines, but they regained a positive light during Pickett's Charge at Gettysburg, where 200 out of 300 were killed including General Armistead.

The 4th Texas

This group of Hispanic soldiers was associated with General John B. Hood and fought at Gaines Mill, Second Manassas, Antietam, Gettysburg, Chickamauga and the Wilderness. They were almost completely wiped out at Antietam.

* * * *

The 15th Alabama

Created in 1861 and commanded by Colonel William C. Oates, this unit fought with Stonewall Jackson and General Longstreet at many of the major battles. They lost almost 350 of 644 men at Gettysburg. Oates later became friends with Joshua Chamberlain, whom he fought against at Gettysburg.

* * * *

The 27th Virginia

This group was also known as the 'Stonewall Brigade' as their commander was General Stonewall Jackson until his death. The unit was wiped out at the Battle of Spotsylvania in 1864.

The Signal Corps

One of the most important groups in the war for both sides, actually did very little fighting. In 1858, Dr. Albert James Myer of New York devised a system of signaling men from long distances. In 1860, Major Myer became the first signal officer in the U.S. Army. His assistant, Edward P. Alexander later resigned to join the Confederate Army and took his knowledge of signaling to their side. Eventually the Union had a Signal Corps of 3,000 men and the Confederates had about 1,500 men. Using a set of flags, they could send information about troop movements from as far as 24 miles away in about ten to thirty minutes.

Ranks, Insignias and Pay

Ranks have always existed in the military. Someone has to be in charge. Most soldiers start out as a Private. Some work their way up the ladder of command. Uniform insignias help soldiers tell who is who on the battlefield and which branch of the service they were in. Each rank has its own pay rate. Confederate soldiers had slightly different insignias and pay.

Rank	Insignia
General	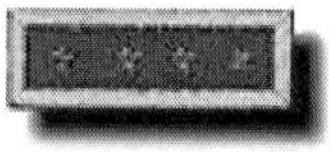
Lieutenant General	
Major General	
Brigadier General	
Colonel	
Lieutenant Colonel & Major	
Captain	
First Lieutenant	
Second Lieutenant	

Rank	Insignia
Sergeant Major	
Quartermaster Sergeant	
Ordnance Sergeant	
First Sergeant	
Sergeant	
Corporal	
Private First Class	No Insignia
Private	No Insignia

The shoulder or arm patches denoting the rank of enlisted men were called chevrons. Today, a single stripe is used to denote a private. During the Civil War, no stripe was used.

The chevrons were different colors to indicate which branch of the military each soldier was in. Red was for Artillery, yellow indicated Cavalry, blue was for Infantry and green indicated the soldier was a Sharpshooter.

When it came to the officer's insignias, the four stars for General was not actually used. Ulysses S. Grant was the first full General since George Washington, but he never wore the insignia during the war. Generals Sherman and Sheridan were promoted to four star Generals after the war.

There were various sleeve insignias used by the Confederate army to denote officers.

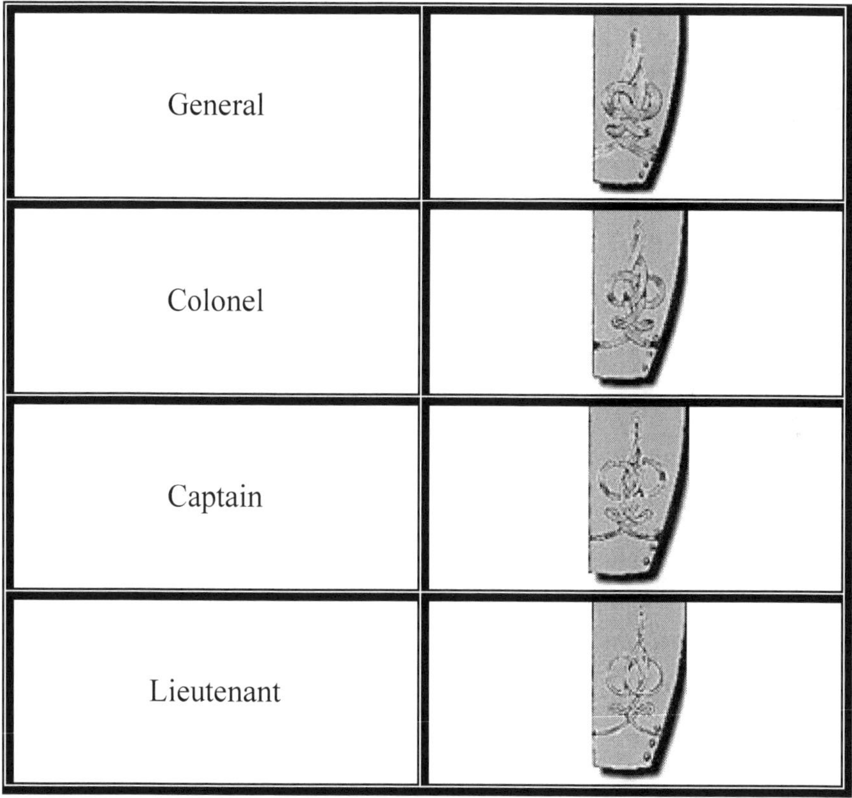

General	
Colonel	
Captain	
Lieutenant	

The insignias were sewn onto the sleeves of the officers. Officers of similar rank, wore the same insignia. For example, Lieutenant General wore the General insignia.

Even after being promoted to full General, Robert E. Lee continued to wear the uniform of a Colonel.

There were various collar insignias for the different ranks of the Confederate military. The Confederates put the rank insignias for their officers right on the collar of their uniforms.

General	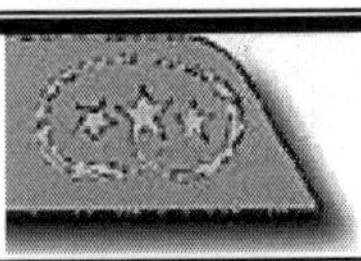
Colonel	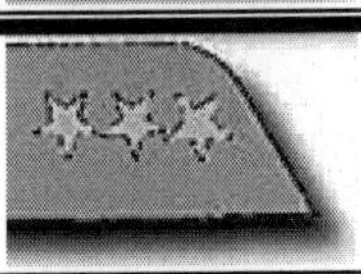
Lieutenant Colonel	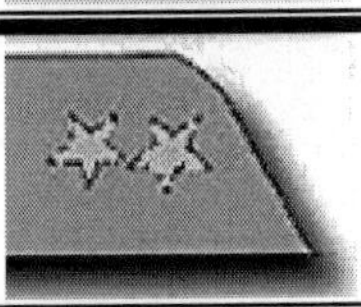
Major	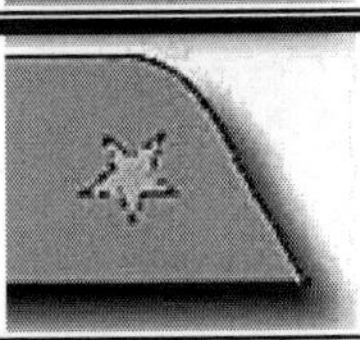
Captain	
First Lieutenant	
Second Lieutenant	

There were various cap insignias for the different branches of the military.

Artillery	
Cavalry	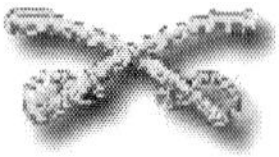
Infantry	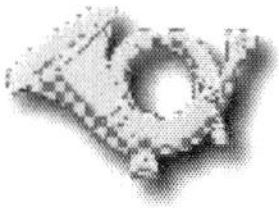
Sharpshooters	
Marine Corps	
Engineer Corps	
Signal Corps	
Ordnance	
Staff Officers	
Generals	

The cap insignias were supposed to be standardized, but quite often, soldiers would purchase or make parts of their own uniforms, creating inventive substitutions.

Monthly pay for Northern, Southern and Modern Soldiers.

Rank	Northern	Southern	Modern
Private	$13	$11	$1274
Corporal	$14	$13	$1662
Sergeant	$17	$17	$1814
2nd Lieutenant	$106	$80	$2783
Captain	$130	$116	$3221
Major	$169	$150	$3664
Lt. Colonel	$181	$170	$4247
Colonel	$212	$195	$5094
Brig. General	$315	$301	$8608
General	$518	$500	$11690

During the Civil War, a Union Private was only paid 13 dollars per month, while a Southern Private was only paid 11 dollars per month. In comparison, a modern private is paid 1,274 dollars per month. During the Civil War, Northern troops were supposed to be paid every two months, but were lucky if they were paid every four months. Confederate troops were lucky if they were paid every six to eight months.

African-American Troops

The United States Colored Troops (USCT) were formed in 1863. 180,000 African-Americans comprising 175 units served in the Union Army during the Civil War. Both free African-Americans and runaway slaves joined the fight. Smaller numbers are said to have fought on the Confederate side including two units in Virginia in 1865.

At first, enrollment was slow. Colored regiments were led by white officers many white soldiers believed that black men lacked the courage to fight. By the end of 1863, fourteen African-American Regiments were in service.

On July 17, 1863, in Indian Territory, the 1st Kansas Colored under General James Blunt ran into a strong Confederate force. After a two-hour battle, the Confederates retreated.

The 1st Kansas held the center of the Union line, advanced to within fifty feet of the Confederates and exchanged fire for twenty minutes until the Southern troops retreated. General Blunt wrote, "I never saw such fighting as was done by the Negro regiment... they make better solders in every respect than any troops I have ever had under my command."

The most widely known battle fought by African-Americans was the assault on Fort Wagner, South Carolina, by the 54th Massachusetts in 1863. The 54th volunteered to lead the assault on the strongly-fortified Confederate position. Frederick Douglass aided in the recruitment of this group and two of his sons served in it. This group was the basis for the movie "Glory."

Although black soldiers proved themselves as soldiers, it was not until June 15, 1864, when Congress granted equal pay for African-American soldiers.

Sixteen African-Americans were awarded the Medal of Honor during the Civil War.

African-American soldiers comprised 10% of the entire Union Army. Approximately one-third of all African Americans in the military lost their lives during the Civil War.

One estimate suggests that between 60,000 and 93,000 blacks, both slave and free, served in the Confederate military in some capacity.

The Confederate Government prohibited enlisting African-Americans in the military. They did authorize payment for African-American musicians to entertain the troops in 1862.

In January, 1864, Confederate General Patrick Cleburne and several other officers proposed using slaves as soldiers in the national army. Southern President Jefferson Davis refused to consider it.

By the fall of 1864, the Confederacy was losing more ground, and some believed that only by arming the slaves could defeat be avoided. On March 23, 1865, an order was issued, allowing slaves to earn their freedom if they fought for the Confederacy.

Only a few African-American companies were raised, and the war ended shortly thereafter.

After the war, many of the USCT veterans received no recognition and no military pensions. Most received no disability pensions until the early 1900s.

The African American Civil War Memorial is located in Washington, D.C. near the national museum on U Street.

The Number of African-American Troops by State

Arkansas	5,526
Alabama	4,969
Connecticut	1,764
Colorado Territory	95
Delaware	954
District of Columbia	3,269
Florida	1,044
Georgia	3,486
Iowa	440
Indiana	1,597
Illinois	1,811
Kansas	2,080
Kentucky	23,703
Louisiana	24,502
Maryland	8,718
Massachusetts	3,966
Michigan	1,387
Mississippi	17,869

Missouri	8,344
Minnesota	104
Maine	104
New Hampshire	125
New York	4,125
New Jersey	1,185
North Carolina	5,035
Ohio	5,092
Pennsylvania	8,612
Rhode Island	1,837
South Carolina	5,462
Texas	47
Tennessee	20,133
Vermont	120
Virginia	5,723
West Virginia	196
Wisconsin	155
At large	733
Not accounted for	5,083
Total	178,895

Ironclads and Submarines

Ironclads were wooden ships covered with thick iron plates to protect against gunfire.

The first ironclad warships were the "turtle ships" of Korea, first mentioned in records from 1413.

The first use of steam-powered ironclads in combat was during the Civil War in October 1861. The CSS Manassas, was an ironclad ram used in combat against the U.S. Navy and proved effective until Northern ships learned to take advantage of its weak armor.

The first engagement of two ironclads was during the Battle of Hampton Roads, in 1862. The Confederate ironclad CSS Virginia and its Union counterpart, USS Monitor, became legendary, and helped to usher in a new age of armored warships. The Virginia was built from the remains of a U.S. ship called the Merrimack.

Among the types of ironclads were monitors, protected cruisers, armored cruisers and armored gunboats.

Combined with steam engine propeller propulsion, the ironclad warship could outfight even the most powerful "three decker."

The age of the ironclad came to an end around 1890, as steel-hulled battleships were developed.

A submarine is like a ship that can operate underwater.

During the Civil War, the North was the first to utilize a submarine. The French Alligator was the first navy submarine, the first to feature an air filtration system, and the first to allow a diver to exit to plant mines on enemy ships. Initially powered by oars, it was eventually converted to a hand-cranked screw propeller. The Alligator was 47 feet long and about 4 feet in diameter with a crew of 20. The sub was lost in a storm in 1863 while under tow to its first combat mission.

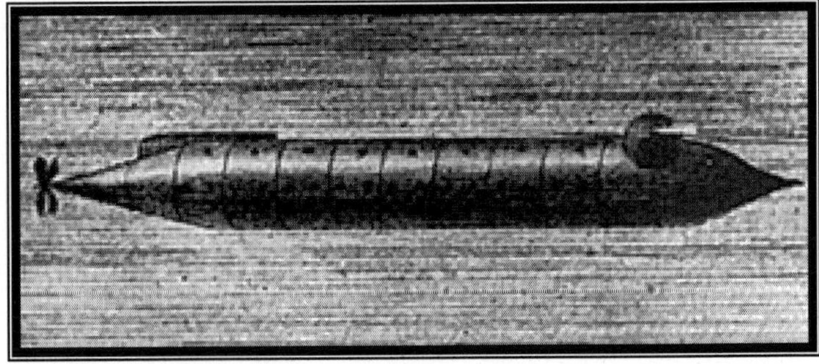

The first Confederate submarine was the 30-foot long Pioneer, which was never used in combat. The Confederacy had several other human-powered submarines including the CSS Hunley. The Hunley was used for attacking the Northern ships, which were blockading the South's seaports.

The submarine had no air supply except what was contained inside the main compartment. On two occasions, the sub sank and the crew drowned. In 1864 the Hunley sank the USS Housatonic. This was the first time a submarine successfully sank another ship, but it sank right after that. Submarines did not have a major impact on the outcome of the Civil War.

During the Civil War, naval battles were common. Most were battles between ships, but that began to change with the invention of the ironclads and submarines.

There were several major naval battles worth noting:

- The Battle of Aquia Creek
- The battle of Island Number Ten
- The Battle of Cockpit Point
- The Battle of Drewery's Bluff
- The Battle of Fort Hyndman

- The Battle of Hampton Roads (The first battle between two ironclads)
- The Battle of Memphis
- The Battle of Tampa
- The Battle of Sewell's Point
- The Second Battle of Sabine's Pass
- The Battle of Mobile Bay

The last shot of the Civil War was fired by the CSS Shenandoah on June 22, 1865.

Civil War Flags

Flags played an important role during the Civil War. Both sides relied heavily on their ability to identify troops quickly.

During the Civil War, flags were considered almost sacred. Making sure your flag (or colors, or standard) was displayed was a matter of honor. In fact, it was an honor to carry the flag into battle. Unfortunately, it was also very dangerous. Although the flag bearer was unarmed, carrying that huge flag was like painting a bullseye on your uniform. It made a very easy and inviting target. Many flag bearers were killed very quickly in battle and nearby men would pick up the flag and proceed to carry it on until they were killed and so on.

The Union and the Confederacy both had their national flags as well. The United States had several flags during the period of the war, as states were still being admitted to the Union. The Confederates also had several national flags as they kept trying to perfect a design. By the time they eventually settled on a design, the war was all but over.

Talking about the flags of the Civil War brings up the topic of what they mean today. For many, the Confederate flag is a source of controversy. For many Southerners, it is a source of pride. For descendents of Confederate veterans, it is historically significant. However, many people today connect the flag to extremist or hate groups such as the Ku Klux Klan. Many would like to see the flag banned or even made illegal. It was only recently removed from government buildings in several Southern capitals.

Another controversy was taking place as this site was being created. An art gallery in Gettysburg was displaying the work of an artist entitled "The Proper Way To Hang A Confederate Flag." The work shows a Confederate flag hanging from a gallows, symbolizing the many lynchings that took place in history. This has drawn criticism from both sides. Many in the North believe the flag should not be displayed, while many in the South believe the flag should not be desecrated. This is a perfect example of how the feelings that were prevalent before, during and after the war are still around today.

In fact, on March 20, 2007, John Schneider and Tom Wopat, the actors that played in the television show, "The Dukes of Hazzard" had a singing engagement cancelled in Ohio because of their connection to the show. During the run of the show, they drove a car called the "General Lee" which had the Confederate flag painted on the roof. The concert promoters felt that the actors connection to what they considered a symbol of oppression, was politically incorrect. Is displaying the Confederate flag insensitive to certain groups? Could banning it be considered insensitive to Southerners? We will leave this to you to decide.

Famous Horses of the Civil War

Horses played a critical role during the Civil War. Both the North and South relied heavily on the strength, endurance and mobility the horses provided on the battlefield. Horses were also relied upon for work and travel and were an essential part of industry.

During the Civil War horses were considered as important as soldiers. They were used to carry messengers, commanding officers, equipment and artillery during the war. Many horses were lost to disease and exhaustion. Because of the value of these horses they often became a target for the enemy.

At one point early in the war, more horses than men were being killed. The average life expectancy for a horse used in the war was about six months.

Northern cavalrymen were provided with horses by the government, but enlisted men who provided their own horse were paid fifty cents extra per day. It is estimated that the Union paid for a total of 840,000 horses during the war.

Southern troops were required to provide their own horses, but were paid forty cents per day for the use. If the horse was killed, the soldier had to find a new one or be transferred to the infantry.

The bodies of dead horses often formed a protective barricade for nearby fighting men. After the battles were over there could be hundreds left lying around, which were usually burned and not buried. The soldier with the worst record for losing horses was General Nathan Bedford Forest, who reportedly had thirty-nine horses killed underneath him in battle.

There was a horse with a bad record for riders also. Four Guillet brothers rode the same horse at different times, each receiving a fatal wound, while the horse survived.

The horses also served another important function, carrying the general. Many generals rode by horseback instead of walking. One reason why the general rode a horse was so that he sat up higher than his troops. This allowed him to monitor progress and potential dangers farther in advance than if he were on the ground.

The following are merely a few of the many famous horses of the Civil War and their riders:

Traveler

Traveler was purchased by General Robert E. Lee in 1862 and is considered by many to be the most famous horse of the Civil War. The horse had been named Jeff Davis prior to General Lee's purchase. General Lee rode Traveler through the majority of the war, including the battles at Gettysburg, Manassas, and Fredericksburg. After the war, Traveler went with General Lee to Washington College. After Lee died, his trusted horse marched in his funeral procession. Traveler is also the "author" of a ghost-written volume that tells about the Civil War as seen through a horse's eyes.

Cincinnati

General Ulysses Grant's favorite war horse was named Cincinnati.. He was the son of Lexington, one of the fastest racehorses of the time and property of General William Tecumseh Sherman. General Grant was given Cincinnati as a gift in 1864 and rarely allowed anyone else to ride him. General Grant rode Cincinnati throughout the war and to his surrender meeting with General Robert E. Lee. The horse stayed with Grant at the White House after he became president and lived until 1878. Grant's other horses included Methuselah, Rondy, Fox, Jack, Jeff Davis and Kangaroo.

* * * *

Lexington

Lexington was the horse of General William Tecumseh Sherman during the Civil War. A famous Kentucky racehorse, Lexington was relied upon for his speed during the war. Lexington carried General Sherman through Atlanta in 1864 and to Washington for the final review of his army. His son, Cincinnati was a gift to General Ulysses Grant.

* * * *

Old Sorrel

This famous horse carried General "Stonewall" Jackson. Old Sorrell was so small that the General's feet nearly touched the ground and was renamed Little Sorrel for this reason. Old Sorrel was purchased by the General at Harper's Ferry in 1861 as a gift for his wife. Jackson was riding the horse when he was mortally wounded at the battle of Chancellorsville in 1863. After his death the horse was sent to the Virginia Military Institute where General Jackson taught.

Baldy

Baldy was the horse of General George Meade. This seemingly indestructible horse was injured at least five times during the war. Baldy carried General Meade through several battles during the war, including Fredericksburg, First Bull Run, Antietam, Chancellorsville and Gettysburg. Baldy outlived General Meade and marched in his funeral procession in 1872.

* * * *

Winchester

This famous Civil War horse belonged to General Philip Sheridan. Its original name was Rienzi. Rienzi was renamed Winchester after a famous ride in 1864, where Sheridan was able to turn defeat into victory. Winchester is preserved at the Smithsonian Institution in Washington, DC. Aldebaron was another horse that General Sheridan rode earlier in the war.

* * * *

Fleeter

Fleeter was ridden by famous Confederate spy Belle Boyd.

* * * *

Black Hawk

Black Hawk was ridden by General William Bate.

Dixie

Dixie was killed at Perryville while being ridden by General Patrick Cleburne.

* * * *

Rifle

Rifle was the cherished steed of General Richard Ewell.

* * * *

King Philip

King Philip was the favorite horse of General Nathan Bedford Forrest, who also rode Roderick and Highlander.

* * * *

Beauregard

Beauregard was ridden to Appomattox by Captain W. I. Rasin and survived until 1883.

* * * *

Joe Smith

General Adam R. Johnson rode a horse named Joe Smith.

Fire-Eater

General Albert S. Johnston was riding Fire-Eater when he was killed at Shiloh.

* * * *

Nellie Gray

General Fitzhugh Lee's horse Nellie Gray was killed at Opequon.

* * * *

Old Fox

Colonel E. G. Skinner rode Old Fox in the First Virginia Infantry.

* * * *

Virginia

General J.E.B. Stuart's horse Virginia is credited with having prevented his capture by jumping an enormous ditch. In addition to this horse, Stuart often rode Highfly.

* * * *

Sardanapalus

Jeff Thompson's favorite horse was Sardanapalus.

Old Whitey

Famous nurse "Mother" Bickerdyke always rode Old Whitey.

* * * *

Almond Eye

General Benjamin “The Beast” Butler rode a horse named Almond Eye.

* * * *

Nellie

Nellie was the favorite horse of General Kenner Garrard.

* * * *

Lookout

General Joseph Hooker cherished his horse named Lookout.

* * * *

Moscow

Moscow was a white horse used in battle by General Philip Kearny. Because the big white horse was an inviting target, Kearny switched to a horse named Decatur and then to Bayard, whose color was light brown.

Slasher

General John Logan rode Slasher into battle. The horse was so fast that an artist painted it with all four feet off the ground.

* * * *

Boomerang

Colonel John McArthur of the Twelfth Illinois Regiment named his horse Boomerang because of his tendency to move backward.

* * * *

Kentuck

General George McClellan's favorite horse was named Kentuck. In addition, McClellan rode a black horse named Bums.

* * * *

Billy

General George Thomas rode a horse name Billy, who was named for General William Tecumseh Sherman.

* * * *

Old Jim

According to records, the last surviving Civil War horse lived until at least 1894. His rider Lieutenant McMahon was killed in action, but Old Jim went back to live in Aiken, South Carolina, entertaining crowds at parades of Civil War Veterans.

Famous Songs of the Civil War

Music also played a critical role during the Civil War. Both the North and South relied heavily on musicians and bands to boost the morale of their troops. Some songs were popular on both sides, but most were specific to either the North or the South.

During the Civil War singing was one of the troops' favorite ways to pass time. Many songs were composed during the war and sung throughout the armies and at home. Many were inspirational marching tunes, while others were sad and sentimental and sung when thinking of home or loved ones. Sometimes, if soldiers liked a tune they heard the opposing side singing, they would write their own lyrics to it.

On the field, fifers played shrill tunes accompanied by drummers beating various beats. Drumbeats originally served two purposes: to tell soldiers what to do, and to keep them in step. Drum calls even issued commands to soldiers. Buglers were crucial in the war because they too were responsible for sounding out commands. These included reveille in the morning as well as field commands such as advance and retreat.

Music has always been an important part of American society. Military bands played at recruitment rallies and their patriotic marching tunes were sometimes a great incentive to inspire young men to enlist.

When volunteer regiments were recruited, a regimental band was usually included as a part of that group. The bands were also needed to play for parades and evening concerts. Union and Confederate armies both had regimental bands. Some brigade bands did accompany their commanders onto the field and played while the battle raged all around them.

Civil War Prison Camps

One of the worst aspects of the Civil War was the treatment of prisoners. For those familiar with its history, the name "Andersonville" creates images of horror almost as bad as those of Nazi concentration camps. The North had its share of equally horrible camps.

Neither side intentionally mistreated prisoners. Neither side expected the war to last long, so they quickly made arrangements to deal with large numbers of men using minimal amounts of money. Prisoners held by the Union were slightly better off as the Southern states were poorer and had less to work with.

In the first two years of the war, there were relatively small numbers of prisoners taken by both sides and they were well treated.

Both sides agreed to a prisoner exchange which operated during the second half of 1862. This stopped when the South refused to return black soldiers and the North refused to consider Jefferson Davis as President of the Confederacy. From 1863 on, both sides were holding large numbers of prisoners that they didn't have the ability to care for.

The most well known of all the Civil War camps is Andersonville. Officially designated Camp Sumter, the prison was located in southern Georgia. More than 45,000 Northern soldiers were confined there between 1864 and 1865. Almost 13,000 men died there and were buried on the prison grounds, which is now a National Cemetery.

The Confederates lacked necessary means for adequate housing. Many men sought protection in crude tents, while others dug holes in the ground for shelter, but most had no shelter of any kind.

No clothing was provided, and many prisoners were dressed only in rags. The prisoners received one pound of corn meal and either one pound of beef or one-third pound of bacon as their daily rations. This was only occasionally supplemented with beans, rice, peas or molasses.

Most prisoners fell victim to dysentery, gangrene, diarrhea and scurvy. The Confederates lacked adequate medical supplies to stop the diseases. More than 900 prisoners died each month for 14 months.

There were about 150 prison camps on both sides during the war.

Conditions in the North weren't much better. The worst Northern camp was Elmira, located in New York a few miles from the Pennsylvania line. Some 12,000 prisoners were confined to a camp meant to hold only 5,000. Two observation towers were built outside the prison walls. For fifteen cents, spectators could watch the prisoners suffering within the compound.

Requests for badly needed medicines were ignored by officials in Washington. The prison earned the nickname "Helmira" as nearly 3,000 of the 12,000 prisoners (25%) died of starvation, mistreatment or disease. All that remains today of Elmira Prison is Woodlawn National Cemetery.

Civil War Hospitals

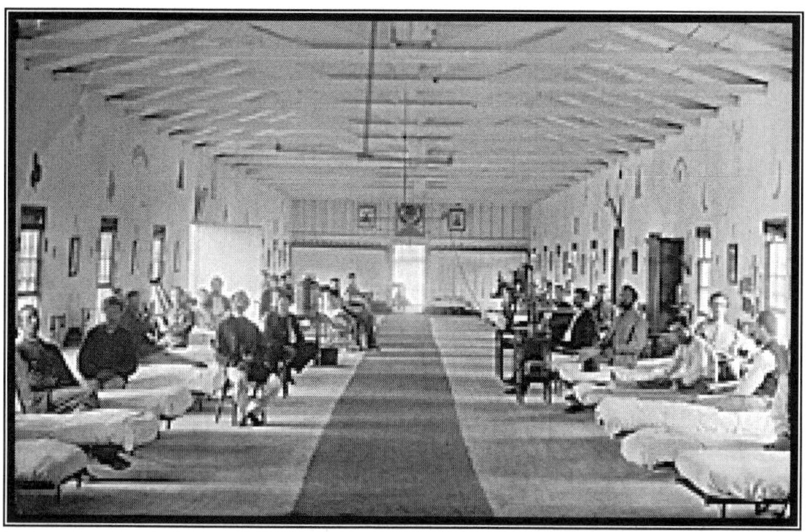

The story of Civil War medicine is upsetting. It is made slightly brighter by the sacrifices and generosity of the doctors and nurses. One reason for the poor conditions was the inadequate preparation for war and the conditions of medicine and public health in general in the mid-1800s.

At the beginning of the war, the United States Surgeon General's office consisted of only 115 surgeons 24 of whom resigned to join the Confederate medical services. The army relied on untrained male nurses. At the beginning of the war, humanitarian, Dorothea Dix, traveled to Washington to offer her services and was appointed Superintendent of Women Nurses.

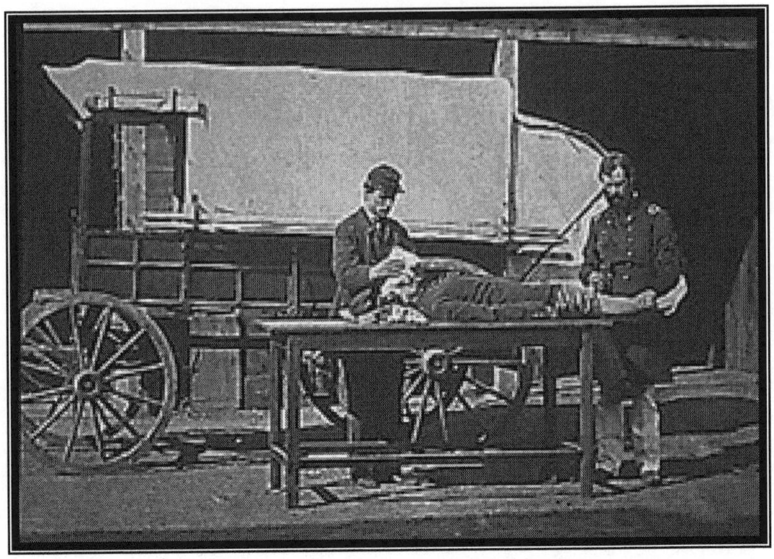

Most field hospitals consisted of nothing more than a tent with a single surgeon, amputating damaged limbs at an alarming rate and throwing them in a pile. Patients received no pain killers or anesthesia. Many died of infection, as there were also no antibiotics and no way to sterilize instruments.

In an inspection of hospitals in the Union Army around 1863, it was reported that a total of 589 hospitals were rated as good and 303 as bad or very bad. Inspections of doctors found 2,727 to be good, while 851 rated as bad!

Reading this, it is not surprising to find that death rates from disease and wounds was higher than from bullets, and that hospitalization was often regarded as a death sentence. Statistics for the Union armies list 67,000 killed in action, 43,000 died of wounds, 224,000 died of disease and an additional 24,000 from "other causes".

Although there are no accurate statistics, it is assumed the situation in the South was even worse.

Civil War Mascots

Wartime animal mascots represented loyalty and bravery. Some of these mascots were an inspiration for the troops and other animals represented pets that the men loved at home. The animal mascots brought enthusiasm to the camp so soldiers would remain happy.

Old Abe

Old Abe was the most famous mascot of the Civil War. In 1860 Chief Sky of the Chippewa Indians captured the eagle. They named him Me-kee-zeen-ce. A little later a farmer named Daniel McCann traded the Indians his ear of corn for the bald eagle. S. M. Jeffers knew that the Eau Clair Badgers wanted a mascot. Jeffers bought the eagle from the farmer for $2.50 and showed it to the Eau Clair Volunteers. They changed the eagles name to Old Abe in honor of President Abraham Lincoln. Old Abe went with the men into battle, and was so use to living with the soldiers that he was allowed to be free and fly above them when they drilled or marched. He was also allowed to walk around camp and sometimes got caught stealing food. Old Abe was involved in a total of 36 battles. Old Abe was a tough bird and lived to be at least 44 years old. Old age did not kill him as the building he lived in caught on fire and he was trapped inside. Although he was not burned in the fire, he inhaled too much smoke and died on February 27, 1904. After is death he was stuffed by a taxidermist.

* * * *

Sallie

Sallie was a Brindle Statfordshire Bull Terrier who was the regimental mascot for the 11th Pennsylvania Volunteer Infantry. Sallie was given to First Lieutenant William R. Terry as a four-week old puppy. She grew up with the men of the regiment. Sallie followed the men on the marches and on the battlefield. At the battle of Gettysburg, Sallie got separated from the men and got lost. She ended up at the Union battle line at Oak Ridge and stood over the dead and wounded. Sallie continued her job through February of 1865, when she was hit by a bullet in the head at the battle of Hatcher's Run, Virginia. She was buried on the battlefield. For her loyalty to the men, Sally was memorialized at the 11th Pennsylvania monument at Gettysburg.

Jack

Jack is one of the best known dog mascots. He was the white and brown Bull Terrier mascot of the 102nd Pennsylvania Infantry. Some volunteer firemen say that Jack understood bugle calls and obeyed the men from his regiment alone. Jack was present at all of the battles in Virginia and Maryland, including the Wilderness, Spotsylvania, and the siege of Petersburg.

* * * *

Dick

The 2nd Rhode Island had a sheep named Dick. Dick was taught tricks by the men. However, he was sold to a butcher for $5 so the men could buy food.

* * * *

Grace

The 1st Maryland Artillery lists the dog Grace as a Unit Mascot. Grace was killed in action.

* * * *

Old Harvey

Old Harvey was a white Bulldog who was a mascot of the 104th Ohio. He served with honor at the Battle of Franklin.

Major

Major was a mutt for the 10th Maine, later recognized as the 29th Maine. Major had a habit of snapping at Confederate bullets in flight and died when he caught one of them. During engagements, Major would growl and bark until the fight was over.

* * * *

Calamity

The 28th Wisconsin Volunteer Infantry, owned a dog that was named Calamity. Calamity would assist the soldiers in foraging missions.

* * * *

Irish Wolfhound

The 69th New York (Irish Brigade) used the Irish Wolfhound as a regimental mascot. He had a picture put on the regimental coat of arms. There were two adopted wolfhounds in the unit which were put in green coats bearing the number "69" in gold letters. They would parade right to the rear of the Regimental Color Guard.

* * * *

Douglas

The 43rd Mississippi Infantry kept a camel named Douglas. Douglas was killed by a bullet during the siege of Vicksburg.

York

York was a Setter, and was Brigadier General Alexander S. Asboth's pet. York usually went into action with his owner.

* * * *

Rifle

Rifle was the cherished steed of General Richard Ewell.

* * * *

Stonewall

The Richmond Howitzers kept a dog named Stonewall who was very admired by the artillerymen. Stonewall was given rides in the safety of a lumber chest during the battles. He was taught to answer to roll calls, sitting on his haunches in line.

* * * *

Other Mascots

- The 3rd Louisiana, CSA, had a donkey. This donkey would push into the commanders tent trying to sleep with his owner, but kept mistaking other officers for his owner.
- The 12th Wisconsin Volunteers had a bear that marched with them to Missouri.
- The 26th Wisconsin Volunteer Infantry had a badger for a mascot.
- The 12th Wisconsin and the 104th Pennsylvania kept raccoons as unit mascots.
- Soldiers of the Richmond Howitzers kept gamecocks as pets.

The Medal of Honor

The Medal of Honor is the highest military honor awarded in the U. S. All branches of the service are eligible to receive the medal and each has its own design. The Coast Guard design has never been awarded. The medal is usually presented to the recipient or survivors by the President.

Although military medals have existed since 1782, the actual Medal of Honor came into existence in 1862. It has changed in appearance several times. The Medal of Honor has been awarded 3,461 times (1,522 during the Civil War), but only 19 people have received it more than once. The only woman to receive the medal was Dr. Mary Edwards Walker.

During the Civil War, the medal was most often awarded for capturing the enemies flag or saving the Union flag.

The Confederates created their own medal in 1862, known as the Southern Cross of Honor. It is unknown how many men received this honor. Because of a shortage of metal during the war, many medals were not awarded.

Civil War Money

During the Civil War, money was important. People needed to pay for things and eat just like they do now. The South decided that since they were a new country, they needed their own currency. Therefore they began printing their own paper money and minting their own coins.

The design of the Confederate coins was very similar to the design of the Northern coins. In fact, back then, the design of many denominations of coins were very similar. One of the reasons was that they were all designed by only two men: James B. Longacre and Christian Gobrecht. All of the Gobrecht coins are referred to as the Seated Liberty type.

Even paper money came in fractional amounts, such as four cents. Back then, paper money functioned as an I.O.U. for the equivalent amount of gold or silver. Each bank could print and issue their own money, but if the bank went out of business, the money was worthless.

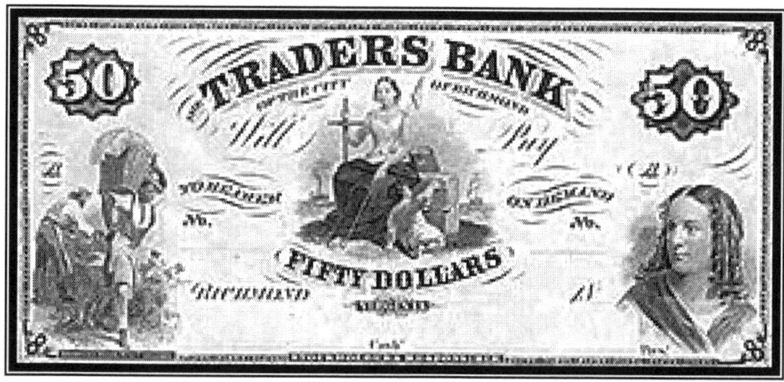

Northern One Cent Piece

The Union One Cent Piece or the Penny as it was known was referred to as the Indian Head Cent. It was designed by James B. Longacre in 1859 and remained in use until 1909, when the Lincoln Cent began.

Northern Two Cent Piece

Yes, there was a Two Cent Piece. It was designed by James B. Longacre in 1864 and is the only coin to begin existence during the Civil War. This was also the first coin to have "In God We Trust" on it. It was discontinued in 1874.

Northern Three Cent Piece

The Three Cent Coin was nicknamed "the Trime." There were actually two types of Three Cent Pieces. The first were minted using silver (1851-1873), but as that metal became more valuable and people began melting the coins down for the value of the metal, the newer coins were made from nickel. This was also designed by James B. Longacre.

Northern Five Cent Piece

The Five Cent Piece was known as the Half Dime instead of the Nickel at this point as it was made from silver, not nickel This coin was designed by Christian Gobrecht and was in circulation from 1837-1873.

Northern Ten Cent Piece

The Ten Cent Piece or Dime was designed by Christian Gobrecht in 1837 and stayed in circulation until 1891.

Northern Twenty-Five Cent Piece

The Twenty-Five Cent Piece or Quarter Dollar was also designed by Christian Gobrecht and was in circulation from 1838 until 1891.

Northern Fifty Cent Piece

The Fifty Cent Piece or Half Dollar was designed by Christian Gobrecht and was in circulation from 1839-1891.

Northern One Dollar Coin

The Silver Dollar coin was designed by Christian Gobrecht in 1840 and remained in circulation until 1873.

Southern One Cent Piece

In 1861, the Confederacy attempted to create its own coinage. Interestingly, they hired a Northerner, Robert Lovett of Philadelphia to design, engrave and mint it. Fearing repercussions, Lovett decided to stop making the coins after only twelve were produced. In 1873, copies of the coins were made from gold silver and copper in limited editions to sell.

Southern Fifty Cent Piece

In 1861, Jefferson Davis himself authorized the creation of a CSA Half Dollar. They were to be minted at the seized U. S. Mint in New Orleans using the U.S. design on the front. The backs were altered to say "Confederate States of America." Only four were ever made.

Children in the Civil War

Children played a role in the American Civil War. In fact, more than 300 Northern Soldiers were under the age of thirteen and a few were under ten.

A lot of the children who joined the war lied about their ages or used fake names. Back then, fighting in a war seemed like a glamorous adventure.

Many of the boys became musicians or drummer boys. The drummer boy's job was to lead the marching troops into battle. Many of them were shot at because they were in the lead.

There are also a few famous examples of children performing heroic deeds during wartime, who were not soldiers.

* * * *

When Johnny Cook was thirteen years old, he served as a bugler with the 4th U.S. Artillery. Just days after his fifteenth birthday, he was involved in the battle of Antietam. Witnessing the cannoneers struck down in battle, he rushed in and took over operations of the cannon. Fighting off three attacks by the South, Johnny was awarded the Medal of Honor. He later joined the Navy and fought on a gunboat until the end of the war. He lived until 1915.

* * * *

Orion P. Howe served as a drummer boy with the 55th Illinois Volunteers. He was shot in the leg during the battle of Vicksburg, but still managed to reach General Sherman with an urgent request for ammunition. Sherman commended the boy for his bravery.

Two drummer boys from the 10th Connecticut Volunteers were present at the battle of Fort Wagner. They happened upon a Confederate Soldier who attempted to fire at them, but his gun did not go off. One of the boys pointed a scope at him, which he mistook for a pistol and he surrendered. They grabbed his weapon and marched him back to camp, as a prisoner.

* * * *

A young boy with the 14th Connecticut Regiment was filling a coffee pot by a stream, when he was surrounded by three Southern soldiers. Instead of retreating, he ordered them to surrender. Thinking that he must not be alone, they did. Seizing one of their weapons, he brought the prisoners back to camp.

* * * *

John Lincoln Clem was only nine, when he ran away from home and joined the 22nd Michigan. Although he was not officially a member, the men chipped in to pay him thirteen dollars each month. At Shiloh, Johnny's drum was hit by an artillery shell and at Chickamauga, Johnny shot an attacking enemy officer. Johnny became known as the Drummer Boy of Chickamauga. Eventually, becoming a courier, Johnny was wounded twice. He retired from service in 1916, having obtained the rank of major general.

In 1864 the young cadets of the Virginia Military Institute joined the battle of New Market to defend against the attacking Union Army. Ten of the 264 cadets were killed defending their school. Every year on May 15th, the school holds a ceremony to honor the brave students.

* * * *

Albert Munson who was fifteen years old, joined the 23rd Massachusetts with his father. During the battle of Roanoke Island, his father was wounded, but Albert continued to drum, using a pistol for a drum stick. Albert marched right up to the enemy, but was shot and killed.

* * * *

Henry Shaler of Indiana captured twenty-five men prisoners at the battle of Gettysburg, more than any other man in the army. He pretended to be a Southern soldier and had the enemy lay down their weapons to help carry wounded. Henry then drew his pistol and marched them all back to his camp.

* * * *

Robert Henry Hendershot was a drummer boy for the 8th Michigan when his regiment was charged with the duty of laying pontoon bridges across the Rappahannock river during the battle of Fredericksburg. Pinned down by sharpshooters, Robert volunteered for the mission, but was denied. He stowed away, by hanging on the back of the boat. submerged in water. His drum was destroyed, but he picked up a musket and captured one of the Confederate sharpshooters.

Lincoln and Davis

Abraham Lincoln was sometimes nicknamed Honest Abe or the Great Emancipator. He was the 16th President of the United States from 1861 to 1865, and was the first President of the United States from the Republican Party. He also personally directed the war campaign, which led the Northern forces to victory over the South.

Lincoln is most famous for his roles in preserving the Union and ending slavery in the United States with the Emancipation Proclamation. However, some abolitionists criticized him for only freeing the slaves under the Confederacy in 1863, and not slaves held in the Union territories. Some claim that the Emancipation Proclamation was merely a ploy to create trouble in the South.

Abraham Lincoln was born on February 12, 1809, in a one-room log cabin on a farm in Kentucky. His parents were Thomas Lincoln and Nancy Hanks. After his death, many sources created the illusion that the Lincolns were dirt poor. However, his father was actually quite wealthy for the times.

When Abe was seven years old, his family moved to Indiana. His mother died two years later and his father married Sarah Bush Johnston. Sarah Lincoln raised young Lincoln as if he were one of her own children.

Abe was self-educated, reading every book he could borrow. He was also skilled with an axe — they called him the "rail splitter" — and a good wrestler.

Lincoln began his political career at the age of 23. He served as a captain in a company of the Illinois militia during the Black Hawk War, although he never saw combat.

He was admitted to the Illinois Bar in 1837, moved to Springfield, Illinois and began to practice law. Abe was one of the most highly respected and successful lawyers in the state and served four terms in the Illinois House of Representatives.

Lincoln married Mary Todd in 1842, who was from a prominent slave-owning family from Kentucky, and allowed his children to spend time there surrounded by slaves. Several of his wife's brothers became Confederate officers.

The couple had four sons: Robert Todd Lincoln (1843-1926), Edward Baker Lincoln (1846-1850), William Wallace Lincoln (1850-1862) and Thomas "Tad" Lincoln (1853-1871). Only Robert survived into adulthood. Abraham Lincoln's bloodline ended when Robert Beckwith (Abe's great-grandson) died on December 24, 1985.

Lincoln was eventually chosen as the Republican presidential candidate in 1860 election because his views on slavery were seen as more moderate than rivals and his simple western origins appealed to the newer states.

On November 6, 1860, Lincoln was elected as the 16th President of the United States, even though he was not even on the ballot in most of the Southern states. Immediately after the election, the Southern states began to secede from the Union. President-elect Lincoln survived an assassination threat in Baltimore, and on February 23, 1861 arrived in disguise in Washington.

In his inaugural address, in a final attempt to prevent the coming war, Lincoln supported a proposed amendment to the constitution, which would have protected slavery in the states in which it already existed. Lincoln opposed a compromise, however, which would have permitted slavery in the western territories.

As the war drew to a close, John Wilkes Booth, a well-known actor and Southern sympathizer, heard that the president and Mrs. Lincoln would be attending Ford's Theatre. Having failed in a plot to kidnap Lincoln earlier, Booth informed his co-conspirators of his intention to kill Lincoln.

The play, Our American Cousin, was a musical comedy. As Lincoln sat in his state box in the balcony, Booth snuck into the box and aimed a single-shot, Derringer at his head, firing at point-blank range. He then jumped from the balcony to the stage below, breaking his leg. Booth managed to limp to his horse and make his escape.

The President was taken across the street from the theater to the Petersen House, where he lay in a coma for nine hours before he died at 7:22 A.M. the next morning, April 15, 1865. Upon his death, Secretary of War Edwin Stanton lamented "now he belongs to the ages."

Booth was hunted down by a military posse twelve days later and shot by Boston Corbett. Four co-conspirators were hanged, while three others were given life sentences.

Lincoln's funeral train carried his remains 1,654 miles to Illinois, even passing through Rochester, New York. He was buried in Oak Ridge Cemetery in Springfield, Illinois.

Lincoln stood 6'3 3/4" (192.4 cm) tall and thus was the tallest president in U.S. history, just edging out Lyndon Johnson at 6'3 1/2" (191.8 cm).

The last surviving witness to Lincoln's assassination was Samuel J. Seymour (1860-1956), who was five at the time.

* * * *

Jefferson Davis (1808 – 1889) was an American soldier and politician, most famous for serving as the one and only President of the Confederate States of America. Before the Civil War, Davis served in the Mexican-American War as a colonel.

Jefferson Davis was born on a farm in Kentucky, less than 100 miles from where Abraham Lincoln was born. Jefferson was the last of ten children whose parents were Samuel Emory Davis and his wife Jane.

Davis had fallen in love with Colonel Zachary Taylor's 16-year-old daughter, Sarah Knox Taylor in 1833. Colonel Taylor did not approve of the match, so Jefferson resigned and married Sarah anyway. The couple both contracted malaria, and Sarah died three months after the wedding.

Jefferson Davis's first political success came in 1844 as he was elected to the United States House of Representatives. He married again in 1845, to Varina Howell.

In the Senate, Davis was chairman of the Committee on Military Affairs. He resigned in 1851 to run for governor of Mississippi, but lost by less than one thousand votes. Davis became Secretary of War under President Franklin Pierce. When Pierce was not re-elected, Davis won another term in the Senate in 1857.

In 1858, he delivered an anti-secessionist speech on board a ship near Boston and again urged the preservation of the Union on October 11 in Faneuil Hall, Boston. Although he was an opponent of secession, Davis announced the secession of Mississippi, delivered a farewell address, and resigned from the Senate in 1861.

On February 9, 1861, a constitutional convention in Alabama named him President of the Confederate States of America. Jefferson immediately appointed a Peace Commission to resolve the Confederacy's differences with the Federal Government, but this was not to be.

On June 1, 1862, he assigned General Robert E. Lee to command the Army of Northern Virginia, the main Confederate army in the East. Davis preferred to remain commander of the military himself and did not assign the job to Robert E. Lee until January 31, 1865, far too late for him to establish a grand strategy that could achieve success.

On April 3, 1865, with General Ulysses Grant ready to capture the Confederate capital of Richmond, Davis escaped for Virginia. Six days later, he proceeded to North Carolina. On April 16, he made a break for Mississippi, but was captured in Georgia on May 10th.

On May 19, 1865, Davis was imprisoned, but was not indicted for treason until a year later due to constitutional concerns. After imprisonment for two years, he was released on bail and the prosecution dropped the case in February of 1869.

That same year, Davis became president of the Carolina Life Insurance Company in Tennessee. After Robert E. Lee's death in 1870, Davis presided over the memorial service. Elected to the U.S. Senate again, he refused the office in 1875.

Over the next three years, Davis wrote *The Rise and Fall of the Confederate Government* . He completed *A Short History of the Confederate States of America* in October 1889. Jefferson Davis died in New Orleans at the age of 81. He is buried in Richmond, Virginia.

The Fourteenth Amendment to the United States Constitution barred from office anyone who had served in the Confederacy. In 1978, Congress removed the ban on Davis. They had taken similar action on behalf of Robert E. Lee in 1977.

The GAR and the UCV

GAR stands for Grand Army of the Republic. It was an organization composed of Union Army Veterans. It was formed in 1866, and by 1890, had almost 500,000 members in every state.

The GAR had a great deal of political power and lobbied for soldier's pensions, retirement homes for soldiers and the creation of Veteran's Day in 1868. The last member of the group died in 1956 at age 109.

A new group was formed in 1881, and called the Sons of Union Veterans of the Civil War (SUVCW). Membership is open to anyone who can prove that they are related to a Union Civil War Veteran.

More information can be found at http://www.suvcw.org

The UCV (United Confederate Veterans) was formed in 1889 and was active through the 1940's. It's function was to preserve the history of the Confederacy, provide for widows and orphans of Southern Soldiers and organize reunions. At its peak, the UCV had approximately 160,000 members.

Two successor groups were formed in 1894 and 1896, called the United Daughters of the Confederacy (UDC) and the Sons of Confederate Veterans (SCV) respectively. These groups are also open to persons who can prove they are descendents of Confederate Veterans.

More information can be found at http://www.hqudc.org and http://www.scv.org

Another organization exists, called the Military Order of the Stars and Bars. It is for descendents of commissioned officers of the CSA. Their website is http://www.mosbihq.org

Weapons of the Civil War

3-in Ordnance Rifle

Weapon: 3-inch Ordnance Rifle
Date of Creation: 1861
Length: 73 in.
Weight: 816 lbs.
Range: 2,300 yds.
Material: Wrought iron
Caliber: na
Interesting Facts: It was extremely durable, reliable, and deadly accurate.

10-pound Parrott Rifle

Weapon: 10-pound Parrott Rifle
Date of Creation: na
Length: 78 in.
Weight: 890 lbs.
Range: 2,000 yds.
Material: Cast and wrought iron
Caliber: na
Interesting Facts: Because it had a longer range, it was helpful in knocking down fortifications at Vicksburg and Atlanta.

1841 6-Pounder Gun

Weapon: 1841 6-Pounder Gun
Date of Creation: 1841
Length: 60 in. tube
Weight: 900 lbs.
Range: 1,500 yds.
Material: Iron
Caliber: 3.67
Interesting Facts: The shot was too small to do much damage. Many were left over from the Mexican War.

12 Pound Howitzer

Weapon: 12 Pound Howitzer
Date of Creation: na
Length: 53 in. tube
Weight: 788 lbs.
Range: It was most effective under 400 yds. It's farthest range was 1,100 yds.
Material: Bronze
Caliber: 4.62
Interesting Facts: It was very mobile and had great firepower.

Napoleon

Weapon: 12 Pound Gun Howitzer (Napoleon)
Date of Creation: 1857
Length: 66 in. tube
Weight: 1,227 lbs. with carriage 2,445 lbs.
Range: 1,700 yds.
Material: Bronze
Caliber: 4.62
Interesting Facts: The design came from Napoleon, a French emperor.

.58 Springfield Musket

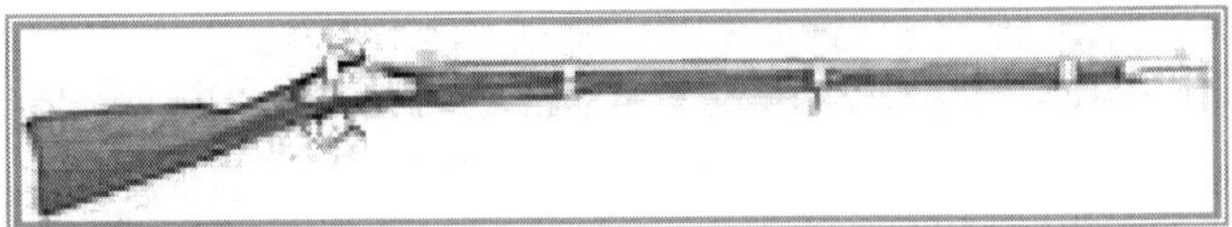

Weapon: .58 Springfield Musket
Date of Creation: 1861
Length: 56 in.
Weight: 9.5 lbs.
Caliber: .58
Interesting Facts: It was the most widely used shoulder arm of the war.

Harper's Ferry Rifle

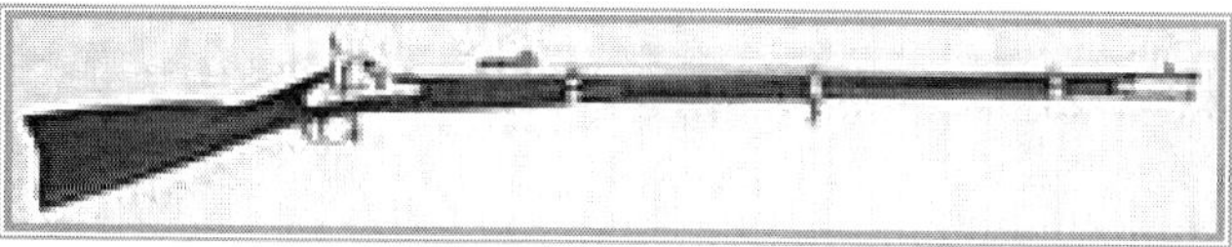

Weapon: Harper's Ferry Rifle
Date of Creation: 1855
Length: 42 in.
Weight: 10 lbs.
Caliber: .69
Interesting Facts: Fired the deadly "minie ball" which was created by Claude F. Minie. The bullet spun when fired, making it very precise.

Spencer Carbine

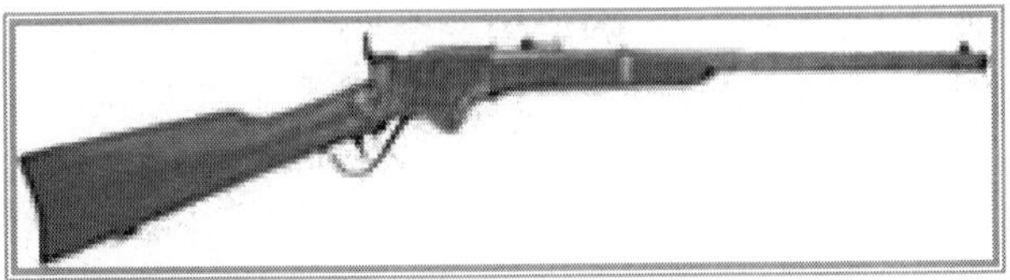

Weapon: Spencer Carbine
Date of Creation: 1860
Length: 47 in.
Weight: 10 lbs. 5 oz.
Caliber: .56
Interesting Facts: It could shoot 14 rounds per minute by moving a lever, compared to 3 per minute by a muzzle loader.

Enfield Rifle

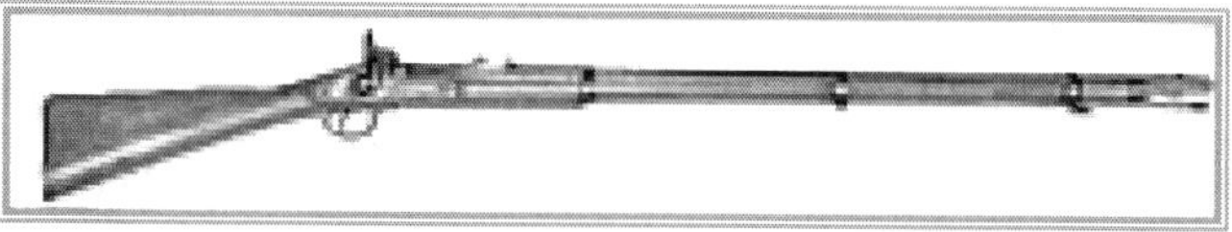

Weapon: English Enfield Rifle
Date of Creation: 1855
Length: 55 in.
Weight: 5.74 lbs.
Caliber: .577
Interesting Facts: The Enfield got its name from the British government.

Sharps 1859 Rifle

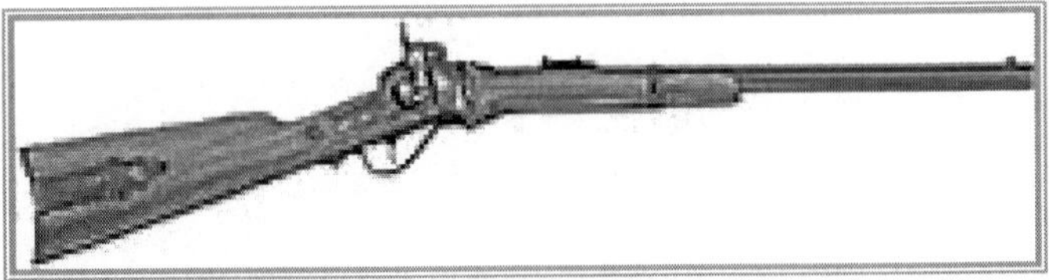

Weapon: Sharps 1859 Rifle
Date of Creation: 1859
Length: 47 in.
Weight: 8 lbs.
Caliber: .52
Interesting Facts: It was developed for mounted troops, since a shorter barrel was easier to handle on horseback.

Whitworth Rifle

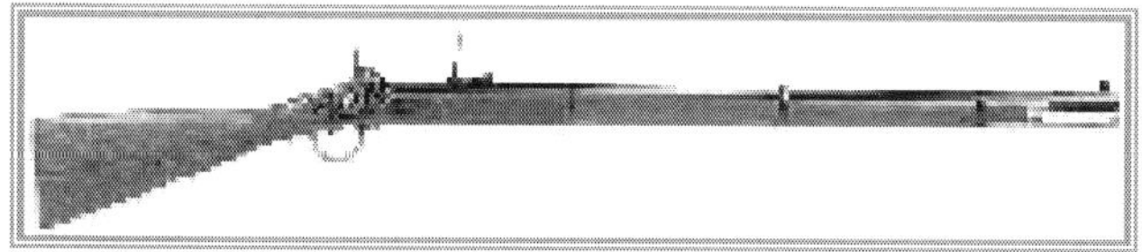

Weapon: Whitworth Rifle
Date of Creation: 1857
Length: 49 in.
Weight: 8 lbs. 15 oz.
Range: 1,800 yds.
Material: steel
Caliber: .44
Interesting Facts: It was mainly used as a sniper rifle with a telescopic site. The bore and slug were both shaped like a hexagon.

Colt 1855 Repeating Rifle

Weapon: Colt 1855 Percussion Repeating Rifle
Date of Creation: 1855
Length: 40 in.
Weight: 9 lbs. 15 oz.
Caliber: .64
Caliber: Sometimes it fired all 6 rounds at once and could explode.

Richmond Musket

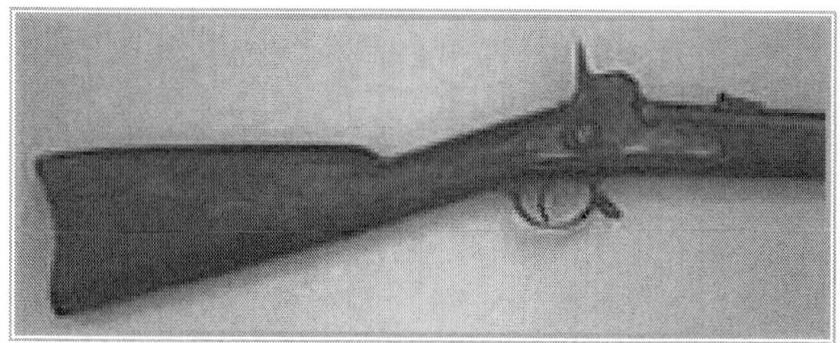

Weapon: Richmond Musket
Date of Creation: 1862
Length: 56 in.
Weight: 10 lbs. 4 oz.
Caliber: .577
Interesting Facts: One of the most inexpensive guns to manufacture.

Cook Cavalry Carbine

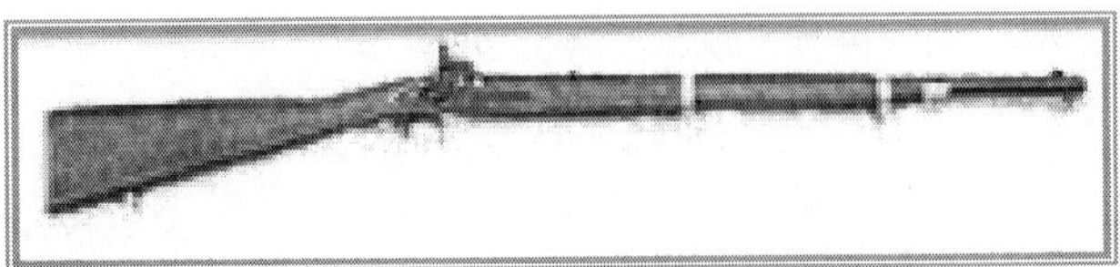

Weapon: Cook and Brother Cavalry Carbine
Date of Creation: 1861
Length: 40 in.
Weight: 7 lbs. 6 oz.
Caliber: .58
Interesting Facts: Made in Athens, Georgia by English immigrant brothers.

Henry Repeating Rifle

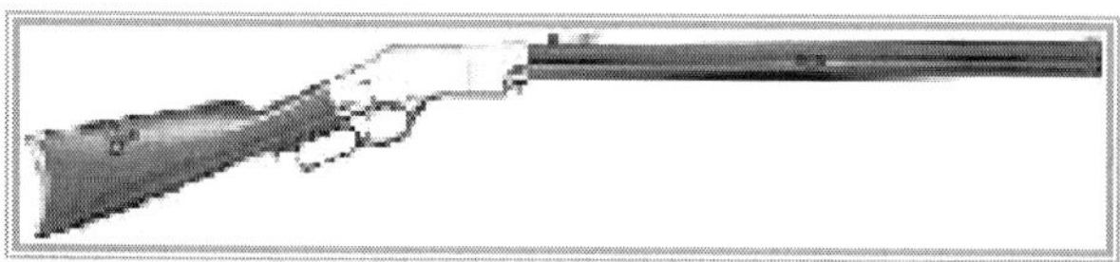

Weapon: Henry Repeating Rifle
Date of Creation: 1860
Length: 42.5 in.
Weight: 6 lbs.
Caliber: .44
Interesting Facts: It used a rimfire cartridge with a metal casing. It also could hold 15 rounds at one time. It was one of the first successful repeating rifles.

Lorenz Rifle

Weapon: Lorenz Rifle
Date of Creation: 1854
Length: 37.5 in. barrel
Weight: 9 lbs. 8 oz.
Caliber: .58
Interesting Facts: The North purchased 225,000 guns just to keep them out of the Confederate's hands.

Maynard Carbine

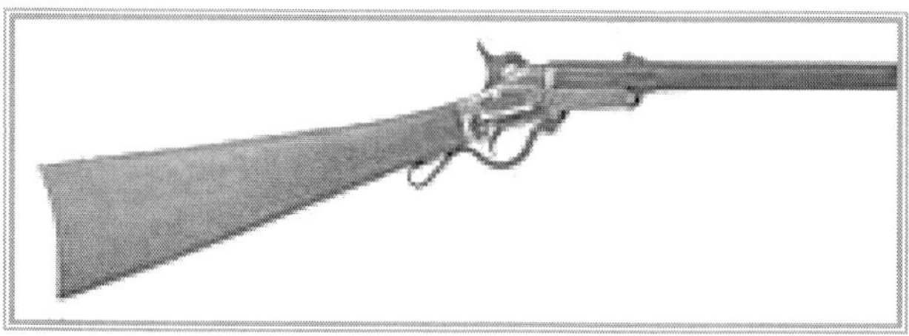

Weapon: Maynard Carbine
Date of Creation: 1861
Length: 40in.
Weight: 9 lbs. 3 oz.
Caliber: .52
Interesting Facts: The Maynard could shoot 12 rounds a minute. It was easily loaded on horseback.

Gatling Gun

Weapon: Gatling Gun
Date of Creation: Designed in 1861, patented in 1862.
Length: 36 in.
Weight: 90 lbs.
Caliber: .50
Interesting Facts: It could shoot 600 rounds a minute and was hand-cranked.

.44 Colt Army Revolver

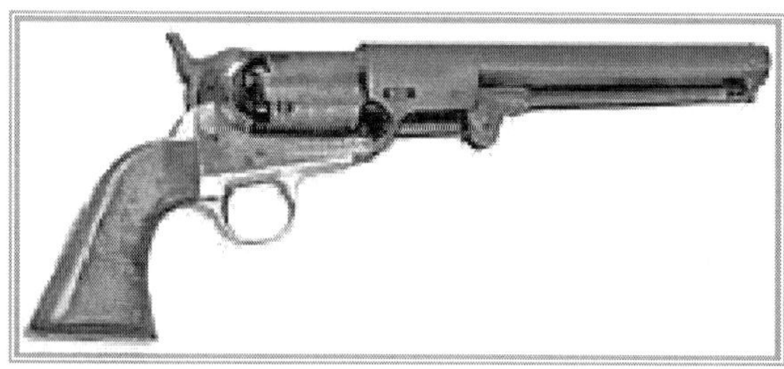

Weapon: .44 Colt Army Revolver
Date of Creation: 1860
Length: 14 in.
Weight: 2.75 lbs.
Caliber: .44
Interesting Facts: Famous for interchangeable parts. It was the most popular sidearm in the Union Army. It was also the most expensive revolver in the war.

Colt Navy Revolver

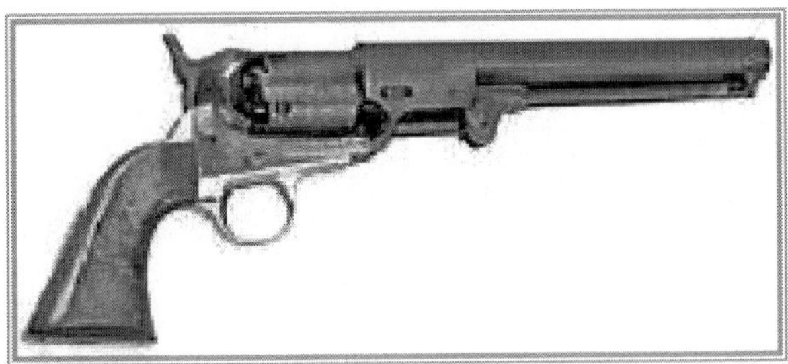

Weapon: Colt Navy Revolver
Date of Creation: 1851
Length: 12 in.
Weight: 2.5 lbs.
Caliber: .36
Interesting Facts: Colt sold this weapon to the Confederates until south fired on Fort Sumter. After that the Union left very few weapons for the south.

Remington Revolver

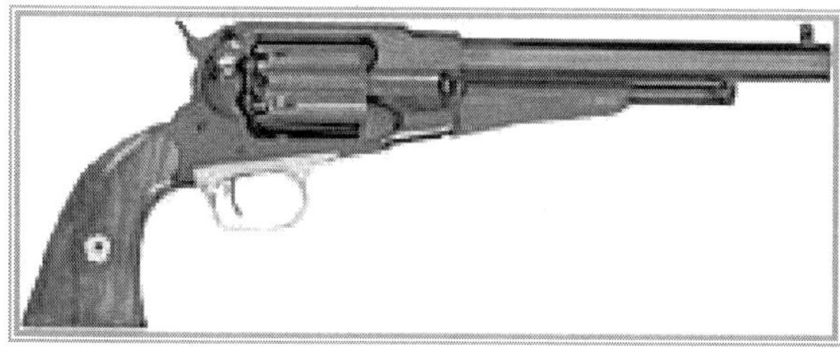

Weapon: Remington Revolver
Date of Creation: 1858
Length: 14 in.
Weight: 2.75 lbs.
Caliber: .44
Interesting Facts: It had a one-piece main frame and one-piece grip.

Starr Army Percussion Revolver

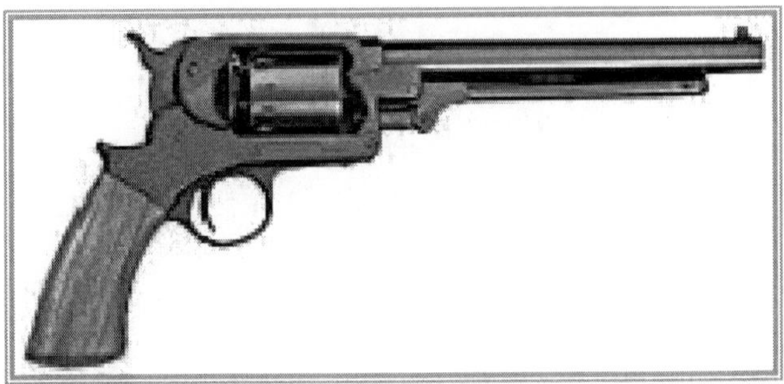

Weapon: Starr Army Percussion Revolver
Date of Creation: 1858
Length: 14 in.
Weight: 2.75 lbs.
Caliber: .44
Interesting Facts: Fired a combustible cartridge.

Lemat Revolver

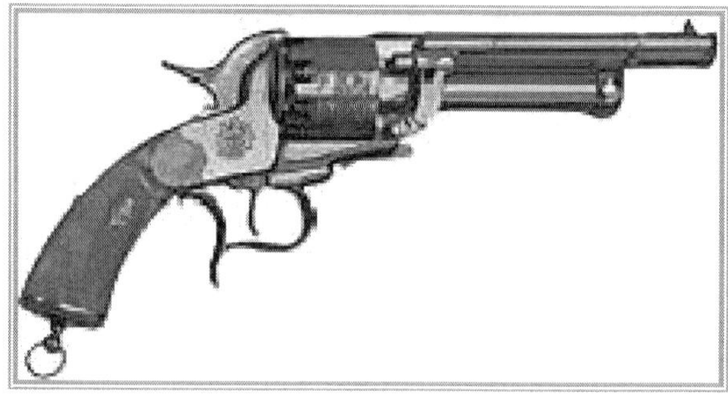

Weapon: French Lemat Revolver
Date of Creation: 1860
Length: 14.75 in.
Weight: 3 lbs.
Caliber: .42
Caliber: It had 2 barrels. The upper fired 9 rounds, while the lower acted like a shotgun.

Schofield Revolver

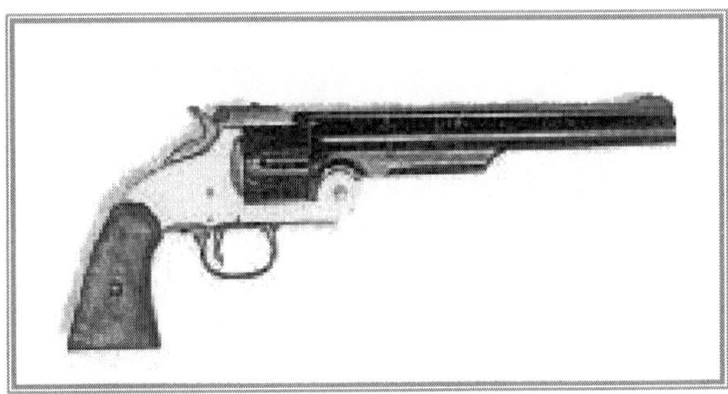

Weapon: Schofield Single-Action Revolver
Date of Creation: 1869
Length: 13 in.
Weight: 2.9 lbs.
Caliber: .45
Interesting Facts: After the war, Fargo agents were known to carry them.

1866 Derringer

Weapon: 1866 Double Barrel Derringer
Date of Creation: 1866
Length: 4.75 in.
Weight: 1 lb.
Caliber: .38
Interesting Facts: It was designed by William Elliot of Remington.

Cogswell Pepperbox Revolver

Weapon: Cogswell Pepperbox Revolver
Date of Creation: mid 1800's
Length: 8.5 in.
Weight: 2 lbs.
Caliber: .476
Interesting Facts: It is a six-shot percussion pistol with a rotating barrel. Additional barrels were carried for quicker reloading.

Kerr Revolver

Weapon: Kerr Revolver
Date of Creation: 1861
Length: 12.25 in.
Weight: 2.2 lbs.
Caliber: .44
Interesting Facts: Made from 1859-1866 by the London Armory Company. They had an exclusive contract with the Confederacy, and when they lost, the company went out of business.

Naval Cutlass

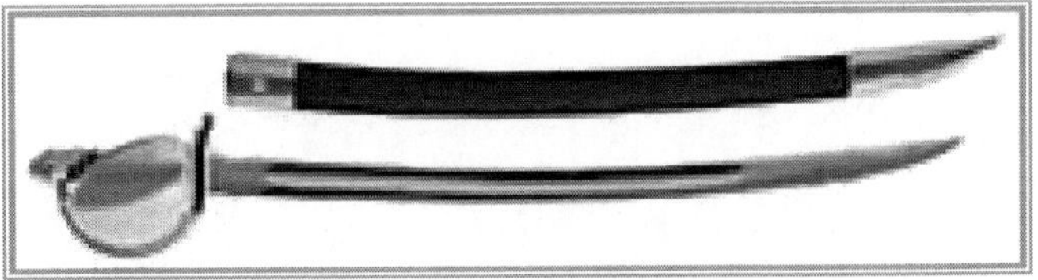

Weapon: Naval Cutlass
Date of Creation: 1860
Length: 32 in.
Weight: 2.75 lbs.
Material: Leather scabbard, the blade came unsharpened.
Interesting Facts: Made for use in close areas. The blade came unsharpened, and owners were expected to sharpen it.

US Cavalry Sabre

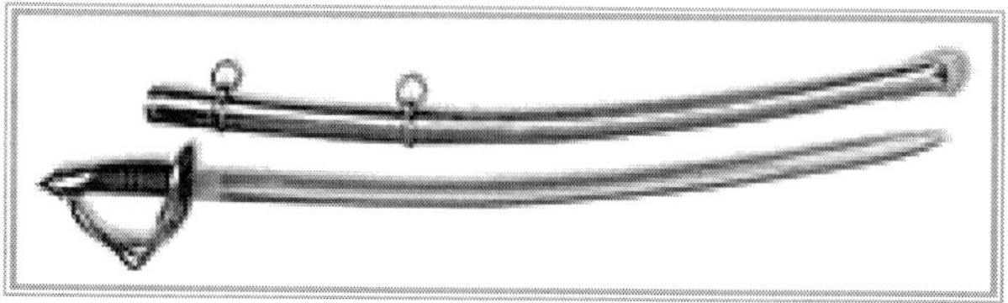

Weapon: US Cavalry Sabre
Date of Creation: 1860
Length: 43 in.
Weight: 2 lbs. 8 oz.
Material: Steel blade and hand guard, scabbard was polished steel.
Interesting Facts: It was the lightest sword in the war.

Confederate Officer's Sabre

Weapon: Confederate Officer's Sabre
Date of Creation: na
Length: 43 in.
Weight: 4.3 lbs.
Material: Steel, leather wrapped grip.
Interesting Facts: Nicknamed after General Joseph Shelby, CSA, who never surrendered.

Cavalry Trooper’s Sword

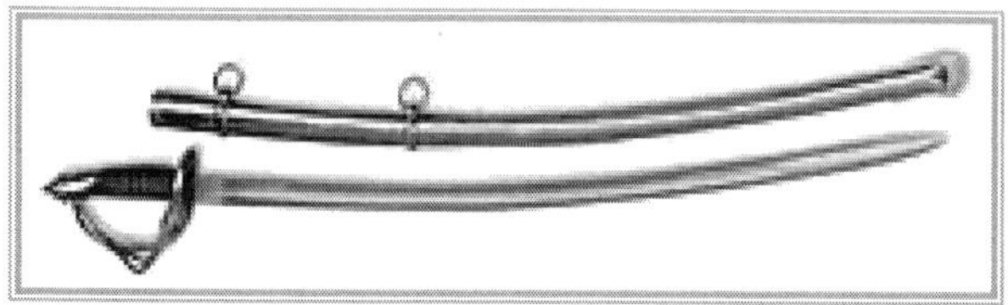

Weapon: Cavalry Trooper's Sword
Date of Creation: 1860
Length: 42 in.
Weight: 4 lbs.
Material: Wood grip with a brass braid and a steel scabbard.
Interesting Facts: The most used sword by troops on both sides.

Fascinating Facts

- "Quaker guns" were logs made to look like guns or cannons to make the enemy think forces were better equipped than they actually were. During the battle of Vicksburg, however, Ulysses Grant actually had his men convert those logs into firing mortars, which they used until they burst.
- 77 of the 425 Confederate Generals were killed during the war.
- Abraham Lincoln and Jefferson Davis served together in the Indian War of 1832.
- Abraham Lincoln had a mild case of smallpox when he delivered his famous 3 minute Gettysburg Address. He was not even the main speaker.
- Abraham Lincoln is the only President of the United States to come under enemy fire while in office. It happened twice, once while on board a tugboat in 1862 and again during a raid on Washington, D.C. in 1864.
- Abraham Lincoln was the first President to wear a beard while in office. After that, it became a tradition to have one for the next nine Presidents.
- Abraham Lincoln's oldest son Robert entered law school at Harvard during the Civil War instead of the army. After grumbling by many, Lincoln arranged for him to become a member of General McClellan's staff with the rank of captain. Robert never actually saw battle and later became Secretary of War and U.S. Minister to Great Britain.
- Adlebert Ames was the last Civil War General to die. He passed away in 1933.
- Admiral Franklin Buchanan fought only two separate days in the war, as he was wounded both times.
- After the battle of Gettysburg, General George Pickett blamed Robert E. Lee for the massacre of his division.
- After the war, many high-ranking Confederates were treated as criminals and denied the right of citizenship. Robert E. Lee petitioned to get his citizenship back in 1865, but it was not restored until 1970.

- Alfred Torbert held commissions in both the Northern and Southern armies at the same time.
- Although there is a misconception that Robert E. Lee was the commander of the Southern forces for the duration of the war, he actually held that post for fewer than ninety days.
- As a boarder, John Wilkes Booth had once occupied the room in which Abraham Lincoln would eventually die in.
- At Andersonville Prison, disease, malnutrition and abuse claimed many lives. An average of 127 men died each day, meaning that bodies were buried at the rate of one every eleven minutes. This death rate was higher than that of most battles.
- At the beginning of the war, the Confederates had about 22,000 rifles and 250,000 muskets. The Union had about 30,000 rifles and 300,000 muskets. Many men still had flintlock muskets from the War of 1812.
- At the beginning of the war, the Confederate Navy did not possess a single gunboat.
- Balloonist Thaddeus Lowe was the first person to direct an attack using aerial reconnaissance on September 24, 1861.
- Bayonets were also rarely used in battle. Enemy fire was usually so heavy a soldier couldn't get close enough to use them. Bayonets were responsible for less than one half of a percent of battle wounds.
- Being a prisoner-of-war was extremely hard during those times. Out of 430,000 prisoners held on both sides, about 260,000 died from disease, hunger or exposure to extreme weather.
- Benjamin Butler was the first Democrat to be made a general by Abraham Lincoln, but lost every battle he fought in.
- By the end of the Civil War, the Union had purchased about 840,000 horses and 430,000 mules.
- Captain Richard Dowling fought off 15,000 Northern troops with only 43 men and six cannons, without losing a single man.

- Carrying the flag was a dangerous job, as it often provided an easy target. On one day alone, at Gettysburg, twenty three flag bearers were killed from just two units.
- Civil War weapons were so inaccurate that it is estimated that for every soldier shot, they needed 240 pounds of gunpowder and 900 pounds of lead.
- Colonel Joshua Howell fought at Yorktown, Williamsburg, Seven Pines, the Seven Days, Fort Wagner and the Bermuda Hundred without a single wound. He died in 1864 after his own horse fell on him.
- During the entire war, both sides each lost only one commander of an army. The North lost General James McPherson of the Army of Tennessee in Atlanta and the South lost General Albert Johnston, who headed the entire western theater at Shiloh.
- Every Southern state except South Carolina had troops fighting for both the Union and the Confederacy.
- For every man who died from battle wounds inflicted in the war, two died from disease.
- Four Northern Generals all came from the same Ohio household. Brothers, Hugh, Thomas, and Charles Ewing all were promoted to the rank of general, as was their foster brother, William Tecumseh Sherman, who also married their sister.
- Frederick Douglass was one of the first people to suggest using black soldiers, but Lincoln did not consider it until much later.
- Future President William McKinley was a member of the Twenty-third Ohio Regiment and saw constant action in places like Antietam, Cedar Creek and Winchester. He often said that he spent four years in uniform without a day in the hospital from a wound or from illness. He was later assassinated in Buffalo, New York by an unemployed mill worker.

- Galusha Pennypacker was the youngest General of the Civil War. He was only 17 years old in 1861.
- General Benjamin McCulloch died at Pea Ridge from a sniper's bullet, without ever having worn a uniform.
- General Edward Hobson captured General John Morgan in 1863. Morgan escaped from the Ohio State Prison four months later and seven months after that captured Hobson in Kentucky.
- General Edwin Sumner was the oldest General in the Civil War.
- General William Tecumseh Sherman was accused by the Northern press of being insane.
- George Barnhart Zimpleman of the Texas Rangers, fought in more than 400 battles, led in the number of horses shot out from under him and suffered two major wounds.
- Gettysburg was called the "high water mark" of the Confederacy. After that battle, General Lee's army was never able to launch another major offensive.
- Gettysburg, Pennsylvania was the site of the largest land battle ever fought in the Western Hemisphere. More than 50,000 men were killed or wounded in just three days.
- Henry Wirz was the only man convicted of war crimes during the Civil War. He was the commandant of the Andersonville Prison in Georgia. He was hanged for starving the Northern prisoners.
- In 1861, the population of the North was 22 million people. The population of the South was only 9 million people. 3.5 million of the 9 were slaves.
- In a similar idea to the "Quaker guns", Admiral David Dixon Porter and his men created a hollow shell of a gunboat, which was unarmed and blew smoke from its smoke stacks. Its purpose was just to distract the enemy from a distance.
- In April 1861, the New York Times assured its readers that the rebellion in the South would last less than 30 days.

- J.E.B. Stuart was still wearing his U.S. Army uniform when he accepted a Southern commission and when he fought at Falling Waters, Virginia in 1861.
- Jefferson Davis served as U.S. Secretary of War from 1853-1857 and introduced the rifle to the military. This would eventually give the North superior firepower to the South.
- Jefferson Davis was so desperate to find commanding officers, that he even promoted men to the rank of general, who had no prior military experience, such as Albert Johnston.
- Jennie Wade was the only civilian killed during the Battle of Gettysburg.
- Jesse and Frank James were members of a local Confederate militia, but eventually gave that up to become renegade raiders.
- Joe Wheeler is the only person to hold the rank of Major General in both the Union and Confederate Armies.
- John Wilkes Booth who assassinated Abraham Lincoln had a brother named Edwin who would later save the life of Lincoln's son Robert.
- Julia Grant is the only wife of a Northern General to be taken prisoner by Confederate forces. General Nathan Bedford Forest had her released immediately.
- Kady Brownell followed her husband to the battlefield near Manassas. She stayed on the field to take care of the wounded soldiers and when the flag bearer was wounded, she carried the flag across the field until she was wounded.
- "Stonewall" Jackson's cousin, General William Jackson's nickname was "Mudwall".
- Many people believe that Robert E. Lee commanded the Southern troops for the entire Civil War. It was actually Adjutant General Samuel Cooper until nearer the end of the conflict.
- Mary Todd Lincoln's family was from the South. She had four brothers who fought for the Confederacy and blamed Ulysses Grant for the southern death toll calling him a "butcher".

- More than 3,000 horses were killed at Gettysburg alone.
- Of the ten officers present at the battle of Fort Sumter, six became major generals.
- One of the worst dressed officers was Confederate General William Jones. He usually wore jeans, a hickory shirt and a homemade coat.
- Only one woman was ever granted a commission in the Confederate Army. Sally Tompkins was made a Captain and ran the Robertson Hospital in Richmond, Virginia.
- Out of more than 1,000 Union Army officers on duty when the war began, more than 300 of them resigned to join the Confederacy.
- Paul Revere's grandson, Colonel Paul Revere was killed during the Battle of Gettysburg.
- Private Edmund Ruffin fired the first shot of the Civil War.
- Private John J. Williams of the 34th Indiana Volunteer Infantry was the last casualty of the Civil War at the Battle of Palmetto Ranch.
- Quite often sounds of cannon fire could be heard from as far as forty miles away. However, there are a number of documented occasions where huge battles appeared to be silent from as few as a hundred yards. One of these occasions was the battle between the Monitor and the Merrimac. This may have been caused by atmospheric conditions.
- Robert E. Lee is the only West Point graduate to complete his degree without receiving a single demerit for violations of the strict disciplinary code.
- Robert E. Lee spent more than a year in Confederate uniform before taking part in a battle.
- Robert E. Lee was originally offered command of the Union Army, but turned it down to join the South.
- Robert E. Lee was the descendent of two signers of the Declaration of Independence, Richard Henry Lee and Francis Lightfoot Lee. His father Harry Lcc was George Washington's cavalry commander during the Revolutionary War. His son "Rooney" was also a Confederate General.

- Samuel Clemens (also known as Mark Twain) joined the Confederate army in Missouri, but only stayed with it a few weeks, before turning to journalism. Eventually, he published the auto-biography of Union General Ulysses Grant.
- Seventeen of the fifty-one Confederate generals who fought at Gettysburg were killed in battle.
- Simon Bolivar Buckner was the last surviving Confederate General. He died in 1914.
- Seven Northern officers became future Presidents of the United States (Andrew Johnson, Ulysses S. Grant, Chester A. Arthur, James A. Garfield, Benjamin Harrison, Rutherford B. Hayes and William McKinley.
- South Carolina was the first state to secede on December 20, 1860.
- Swords were rarely used for more than decorative purposes during the war. Officers would wave them to urge their troops on and use them to cook food over the fire. General "Stonewall" Jackson used his so little, that it literally rusted to his scabbard.
- The 1st Maine Heavy Artillery was the regiment with the highest number of officers killed - 32.
- The 5th New Hampshire Infantry was the regiment with the most battle deaths - 195.
- The Battle of Picacho Pass was fought in Arizona, making it the battle fought the farthest west.
- The Civil War began on April 12, 1861 and officially ended on April 26, 1865, but the final surrender did not take place until November 6th, when the Confederate warship, Shenandoah was captured in Liverpool, England.
- The Civil War introduced many firsts including naval torpedoes, machine guns, repeating rifles, battlefield photographs, the income tax, the Medal of Honor, a snorkel breathing device, a periscope for trench warfare, land mine fields, flame throwers, aerial reconnaissance (from balloons), the first African-American Army Officer and many more.

- The Civil War lasted for 1,396 day, from 1861 until 1865. Approximately 623,000 soldiers died in about 10,455 military "events".
- The Confederate Navy had no ships in 1861 and eventually had 18 ships built in England.
- The Confederate Navy used the world's first successful submarine in 1864. The Hunley sank three times drowning her crew each time.
- The Confederates, as a secret weapon designed an iron-casting to resemble a lump of coal and filled it with explosives. This was then placed in a Union coal bin and would explode when placed in the fire.
- The CSS Shenandoah was still fighting at sea for more than six months after Lee surrendered. Its captain finally surrendered on November 6, 1865 in Liverpool, England.
- The fighting in Spotsylvania was so intense that a white oak tree, almost two feet in diameter was cut down by bullets.
- The first aircraft carrier was a special boat that hauled hot air balloons.
- The first battle of the Civil War was at Fort Sumter in South Carolina. 3,000 shells were fired over 38 hours, but not a single man was killed on either side.
- The first capital of the Confederacy was Montgomery, Alabama.
- The first Confederate General killed in action was Robert Garnett on July 13, 1861 in Corrick's Ford, Virginia.
- The first major battle of the Civil War (Manassas or Bull Run) took place on the property of Wilmer McLean. After a cannonball crashed through his house, he moved his family to the town of Appomattox Court House to escape the fighting. In a strange coincidence, one of the last battles of the Civil War took place on his new property. There Robert E. Lee would surrender to Ulysses S. Grant in the parlor of his home.

- The first person killed in the Civil War was Colonel Elmer E. Ellsworth of New York on May 24, 1861 in Alexandria, Virginia.
- The largest cavalry battle of the war took place at the Battle of Brandy Station.
- The men of the Seventy-ninth New York wore kilts as uniforms.
- The Northern flag is known as the "Stars and Stripes." The Southern flag is known as the "Stars and Bars."
- The only officer know to have directed his troops while lying in a bed in the back of a wagon was Southern Colonel Eppa Hunter, who had become disabled after surgery.
- The Shenandoah Valley was the most fought over area during the war. Winchester, Virginia changed hands an amazing 76 times.
- The Union had only about 16,000 troops at the beginning of the war, but almost 3,000,000 by the time the war ended.
- The Union Navy had only 42 ships in 1861. By 1865, they had nearly 700.
- The youngest soldier was Edward Black who was a 9 year old musician.
- There was another Abraham Lincoln during the Civil War who was on the opposite side. Private Abraham Lincoln was a Confederate deserter from Virginia.
- There were almost 6,000 battles and skirmishes during the Civil War. Almost 600 were considered full battles, while about 35 of them were considered major battles.
- There were two Brigadier Generals named Henry H. Sibley. Both served in the west. However, one fought for the North and the other for the South.
- Twenty Civil War Generals graduated from West Point in 1841.
- Ulysses Grant was introduced to his wife Julia Dent by her cousin, Southern General James Longstreet.

- Union General George Custer was known as one of the best dressed officers of the war. He had his own tailor make a uniform of blue velvet heavily trimmed in gold.
- Walter Williams was the last reported living Civil War Veteran. He died on December 19, 1959 at the age of 117.
- "Wild Bill" Hickock claimed to have killed fifty Confederates with only fifty shots.
- William Dixon Porter, who commanded river boats near Kentucky wanted action so badly that he tried to provoke the Confederates into a fight by hoisting insulting cartoons or taunts on a special mast on his boat.
- William Pender was the youngest General killed in the Civil War at only 29 years old.

Haunted Sites

More Americans died in the Civil War than in any other conflict, and almost all of them were killed on American soil. Almost since the days of the war itself, stories have circulated of strange, unexplained phenomenon surrounding the areas where conflict occurred.

Many people believe that the "spirit" is the true essence of the person and the body is just the vessel it lives in for a relatively short time. Why then, isn't it possible for these spirits to manifest themselves using sight, sound, or touch? What happens when a person dies? Is this life all there is, or a preparation for the next phase of existence?

For some reason, spirits seem to linger around places of great emotional turmoil. If an individual dies a violent death, will he remain behind? Or can the presence of these spirits be explained by ripples in time?

Many people believe that these Civil War sites are haunted as well as hallowed. Many of the towns where battles took place offer "Ghost Tours." The tours are legitimate in that they tell the history of the site and recall experiences by other people. It is unknown however, if anyone on any of these tours has actually seen a real apparition.

The building on the right is the George house, where General Reynolds was carried and later died. His ghost has been spotted there by several different groups of people.

Many reenactors have also reported hearing mysterious shots, smelling smoke, or seeing spirits. Some have suggested that the psychic energy released from reenacting these tragic events has either allowed the spirits to manifest themselves or that the reenactors frame of mind contributes to them seeing these things.

There are many photographs of "spirit activity" in existence. The majority of these consist of foggy images or glowing orbs. The legitimacy of many of these photographs have been challenged as there are those who would create a hoax for profit, but many of the pictures remain unexplained.

In fact, on his last trip to Antietam, while photographing Burnside Bridge for this project, one of Mr. H.'s pictures clearly shows a glowing orb. Is this a restless spirit or a water drop on the lens? We will leave it to you to decide.

There are many interesting books, videos and websites on this subject to help you explore further. If you do get to Gettysburg, we encourage you to have fun on one of the many Ghost Walk Tours. Enjoy!

Reunions

Since the end of the Civil War, small groups of veterans have held reunions. However, there have been several large scale reunions over the years.

Among the most notable get-togethers have been the ones at Gettysburg in 1888, 1913 and 1938. To celebrate the 25th anniversary of the great battle, many veterans gathered at the site. A decision was made to hold a reunion every 25 years, and another was organized by the state of Pennsylvania in 1913 to celebrate the 50th anniversary.

During the 1913 Reunion, over 54,000 veterans attended, many of them aging and frail. The youngest veteran was 61 and the oldest was 112. It was an emotional event, commemorated by the shaking of hands by both the Northern and Southern troops over a stone wall, and a reenactment of Pickett's Charge. Most of the event was civil, however, there was an incident where a veteran attacked another with a fork.

The Reunion of 1938 was promoted as "The Last Reunion of the Blue and Gray." By that time, 75 years had passed and most of the remaining veterans, many of whom had only been boys at the time of the battle, were in their 90's or even older than 100. Still, almost 2,000 were able to attend. Several of the veterans died in the extreme heat. The event was marked by the dedication of the Peace Memorial by Franklin D. Roosevelt. It was an eternal flame that still burns brightly today and is a popular tourist attraction.

There was never to be a 100th anniversary reunion, as the last veteran died in 1956, just 7 years before it would have taken place. The last Civil War widow is still living. She was married to a much older Southern Gentleman.

Video footage of the later events actually exists.

Reenacting

A reenactment is an attempt to recreate an event. Civil War reenactors are people who recreate either Civil War battles or encampment settings.

Reenactments can be either small encampments with three or four members, or major reenactments, such as restaging the battle of Gettysburg with 20,000 people.

A living history is a demonstration for the public that portrays the life of the typical Civil War soldier or civilian. These often include weapons demonstrations, but not battles.

Public demonstrations are small mock battles done by small groups to stimulate public interest.

Tactical battles are usually not open to the public as they are non-scripted attempts to tactically outwit the opposing team.

A scripted battle is one that is planned out in advance and based upon real historical events. This is the most common type of reenactment open to spectators.

Reenacting can be fun and rewarding for the whole family. When you tour an encampment, you even see children dressing the part and participating. Families often camp and live as people did during those times for an entire weekend.

Some people participate because they are history buffs and want to be part of historical events, while others enjoy the escapism aspect.

Reenacting is an expensive hobby. Purchasing uniforms, supplies and weapons can be very costly depending on how deeply one chooses to get into it.

Our group was fortunate to be able to attend a half-dozen different reenactments in our area and participate in two of them.

Civil Wars of the World

The United States is not the only country in the world to experience a civil war. In fact, such conflicts are common.

Here is an chronological list of civil wars of other nations.

Warring States Period of China	475 BC - 221 BC
Civil War of Carthage	309 BC - 308 BC
Mercenary War	241 BC - 237 BC
Brothers Civil War	1067 - 1072
Anarchy of England	1135 - 1153
Genpei War of Japan	1180 - 1185
Great Feudal War of Russia	1425 - 1453
English Wars of the Roses	1455 - 1485
Onin War of Japan	1467 - 1477
Sengoku Period of Japan	1467 - 1615
French Wars of Religion	1562 - 1598
Rokosz of Zebrzydowski - Poland	1606 - 1609
English Civil War	1642 - 1651
Scottish Civil War	1644 - 1652
Zulu Civil War	1817 - 1819
Taiping Civil War of China	1851 - 1864
War of Reform of Mexico	1857 - 1861
American Civil War	1861 - 1865
Klang War	1867 - 1874
Boshin War of Japan	1868 - 1869
Jementah Civil War	1879
Russian Civil War	1917 - 1921
Finnish Civil War	1918
Irish Civil War	1922 - 1923
First Chinese Civil War	1928 - 1937

Second Chinese Civil War	1945 - 1949
Vietnamese Civil War	1930 - 1975
Austrian Civil War	1934
Spanish Civil War	1936 - 1939
Greek Civil War	1946 - 1949
Paraguayan Civil War	1947
Costa Rica Civil War	1948
Korean Civil War	1950 - 1953
Indonesian Civil War	1965 - 1966
Nigerian Civil War	1967 - 1970
Pakistan Civil War	1971
Lebanese Civil War	1975 - 1990
Mozambican Civil War	1975 - 1992
Sandanista Civil War	1979 - 1989
Salvadoran Civil War	1979 - 1991
Yugoslav Wars	1991 - 2000
Afghan Civil War	1992 - 2001
First Congo War	1996 - 1997
Second Congo War	1998 - 2002

Battlefield Preservation

The Civil War battlefields in our nation are being destroyed. The hallowed ground, where almost one million of our American ancestors died or were wounded, is being paved over for drug stores, pizza places, supermarkets and houses.

Almost twenty percent of these battlefields have already been destroyed forever, denying them to future generations. Only 15 percent are protected by the government. Fortunately, there is one organization working to preserve these battlefields: The Civil War Preservation Trust.

The Civil War Preservation Trust is America's largest non-profit group dedicated to the preservation of our country's Civil War battlefields. The organization was formed from the Association for the Preservation of Civil War Sites and the Civil War Trust in 1999.

The group also promotes tourism and educational programs to inform the public about the Civil War, the conflicts that caused it and the roles that these battlefields played in directing the course of our nation's history. Teachers may sign up for classroom memberships for only 25 dollars.

There are also curriculum CDs available to teachers free of charge and the Trust has a classroom visitor listing to get reenactors out to schools at http://www.civilwar.org/historyclassroom/hc_classvisitors.htm .

Since its creation, the Civil War Preservation Trust has saved approximately 20,000 acres of Civil War battlefield land at 81 different battlefields in 19 states. The group has 63,000 members including our team.

To learn more about the work that this group is doing to preserve our national history, click on the link to their website below. You may also call or write them to become involved in letter writing campaigns or to make a donation. Hopefully, you will have the opportunity to visit one of these historic sites in your lifetime.

The Civil War Preservation Trust
1331 H Street N.W. Suite 1001
Washington, D.C. 20005
202-367-1861

info@civilwar.org

Movies About the Civil War

There have been many films produced about the Civil War. Some have been fictional, while others have portrayed actual people and events. Here are a few along with the year they were made.

The Birth of a Nation - 1915
The General - 1927
Gone With the Wind - 1939
They Died With Their Boots On - 1942
The Red Badge of Courage - 1951
Drums in the Deep South - 1951
Friendly Persuasion - 1956
The Great Locomotive chase - 1956
The Horse Soldiers - 1959
Shenandoah - 1965
The Good, the Bad and the Ugly - 1966
Rio Lobo - 1970
The Outlaw Josey Wales - 1976
The Blue and the Gray - 1982
The North and the South - 1985
Glory - 1989
Gettysburg - 1993
Pharaoh's Army - 1995
Andersonville - 1996
Ride With the Devil - 1999
Gods and Generals - 2003
Cold Mountain - 2003
Wicked Spring - 2005

Books About the Civil War

Fiction:

- Banks, Sara Harrell – Abraham's Battle: A Novel of Gettysburg
- Bartoletti, Susan Campbell – No Man's Land
- Beatty, Patricia – Charley Skedaddle
- Beatty, Patricia – Turn Homeward Hannalee
- Blackwood, Gary - Second Sight
- Clapp, Patricia – The Tamarack Tree
- Collier, James and Lincoln – With Every Drop of Blood
- Cornwell, Bernard - The Starbuck Chronicles
- Crane, Stephen – The Red Badge of Courage
- Doctorow, E.L. – The March
- Faulkner, William - Absalom, Absalom!
- Faulkner, William - The UnVanquished
- Fleischman, Paul – Bull Run
- Foote, Shelby - Shiloh
- Frazier, Charles – Cold Mountain
- Gillem, Harriette – Forty Acres and a Mule
- Hesse, Karen – A Light in the Storm: The Civil War Diary of Amelia Martin, Fenwick Island, Delaware, 1861
- Hesse, Karen – When Will This Cruel War Be Over? The Civil War Diary of Emma Simpson, Gordonsville, Virginia, 1864
- Hunt, Irene – Across Five Aprils
- Immel, Mary Blair – Captured! A Boy Trapped in the Civil War
- Jackson, N.R. & Lunn, Janet – The Root Cellar
- Jakes, John - The Titans
- Jakes, John - Love and War
- Johnston, Mary - The Long Roll
- Keith, Harold – Rifles for Watie
- Lyons, Mary E. & Branch, Muriel – Dear Ellen Bee: A Civil War Scrapbook of Two Union Spies

- McCann, William - Ambrose Bierce's Civil War
- McPherson, James M. – Fields of Fury: The American Civil War
- Mitchell, Margaret – Gone With the Wind
- Mrazek, Robert J. – Stonewall's Gold: A Novel of the Civil War
- Murphy, Jim – The Boy's War
- Osborne, Mary Pope – A Time to Dance: Virginia's Civil War Diary
- Osborne, Mary Pope – Civil War on Sunday
- Osborne, Mary Pope – My America: My Brother's Keeper; Virginia's Civil War Diary, Book One
- Paulsen, Gary – Soldier's Heart
- Pinkney, Andrea Davis – Silent Thunder
- Polacco, Patricia – Pink and Say
- Reed, Ishmael – Flight to Canada
- Reeder, Carolyn – Shades of Gray
- Reit, Seymour – Behind Rebel Lines: The Incredible Story of Emma Edmonds; Civil War Spy
- Rinaldi, Anne – Amelia's War
- Rinaldi, Anne – An Acquaintance with Darkness
- Rinaldi, Anne – In My Father's House
- Rinaldi, Anne - The Last Silk Dress
- Ripley, Alexandra - Charleston
- Safire, William - Freedom
- Shaara, Jeffrey – Gods and Generals
- Shaara, Jeffrey – The Last Full Measure
- Shaara, Michael – The Killer Angels
- Smith, Pamela Hill – Voice From the Border
- Street, James – By Valour and Arms
- Styple, William B. – The Little Bugler
- Turtledove, Harry - Fort Pillow
- Verne, Jules – North Against South
- Vidal, Gore - Lincoln
- Willis, Connie - Lincoln's Dreams
- Wisler, G. Clifton – Mr. Lincoln's Drummer
- Wisler, G. Clifton – Red Cap

Non-Fiction:

- Baker, Jean H. - Mary Todd Lincoln, A Biography
- Bearss, Edwin C. - The Vicksburg Campaign
- Beller, Susan Provost and McElderry, Margaret - Never Were Men So Brave: The Irish Brigade During the Civil War
- Bennet, Barbara - Stonewall Jackson: Lee's Greatest Lieutenant
- Bishop, Jim - The Day Lincoln Was Shot
- Boatner, Mark M. III - The Civil War dictionary
- Bolotin, Norman - The Civil War A to Z: A Young Reader's Guide to Over 100 People, Places and Points of Interest
- Brill, Marlene Targ - Diary of a Drummer Boy
- Catton, Bruce - America Goes to War, The Civil War and Its Meaning in American Culture
- Catton, Bruce - The Army of the Potomac
- Catton, Bruce - The Centennial History of the Civil War
- Chamberlain, Joshua Lawrence - Bayonet Forward! My Civil War Reminiscences
- Chang, Ina - A Separate Battle: Women and the Civil War
- Chesnutt, Mary Boykin - Mary Chesnut's Civil War
- Davis, Burke - The Civil War: Strange and Fascinating Facts
- Davis, Burke - To Appomattox, Nine April Days, 1865
- Davis, William - The Civil War Cookbook
- Dolan, Edward F. - American Civil War: A House Divided
- Foote, Shelby - The Civil War, A Narrative
- Freeman, Douglas Southall - Lee's Lieutenants, A Study in Command
- Garrison, Webb - Civil War Curiosities: Strange Stories, Oddities, Events, and Coincidences
- Hearn, Chester G. - Admiral David Dixon Porter, The Civil War Years
- Herbert, Janis - The Civil War for Kids: A History With 21 Activities
- Hill, Lois - Poems and Songs of the Civil War
- Johnson, Robert Underwood and Clarence Clough Buel - Battles and Leaders of the Civil War

- Jouineau, Andrew - Officers and Soldiers of the American Civil War
- Kantor, MacKinlay - Andersonville
- Kantor, MacKinlay - Gettysburg
- Kennedy, Frances H. - The Civil War Battlefield Guide
- Long, E. B. - The Civil War Day by Day, An Almanac 1861-1865
- McPherson, James - Abraham Lincoln and the Second American Revolution
- McPherson, James - Battle Cry of Freedom, The Civil War Era
- McPherson, James - Drawn With the Sword, Reflections on the American Civil War
- Moore, Kay - If You Lived at the Time of the Civil War
- Oates, Stephen B. - A Woman of Valor, Clara Barton and the Civil War
- Priest, John Michael - Antietam, The Soldier's Battle
- Sherman, William Tecumseh - Memoirs of General W. T. Sherman
- Stuart, James Elwell Brown - The Letters of General James E. B. Stuart
- Swank, Wallbrook D. - Ballads of the North and South in the Civil War
- Time Life Books - The Civil War
- U. S. War Department - The War of the Rebellion: A Compilation of the Official Records of the Union and Confederate Armies
- Whitelaw, Nancy - Clara Barton: Civil War Nurse
- Whitman, Walt - Walt Whitman's Civil War
- Williams, Edward F. III - Great American Civil War Trivia
- Woolsey, Jane Stuart - Hospital Days, Reminiscences of a Civil War Nurse
- Zeinart, Karen - Those Courageous Women of the Civil War

Glossary

abatis	Trees sharpened at one end, facing toward the enemy to prevent an advance.
abolition	To put an end to slavery.
abolitionist	Someone who wants to eliminate slavery.
ambulance	From the French term meaning "walking hospital". A horse cart used to transport wounded soldiers from the battlefield to a hospital tent.
amputate	To remove a severely damaged limb (usually an arm or leg).
Anaconda Plan	Plan by which the North would encircle the South, cutting off supplies and slowly crush it.
army	The largest group of soldiers in the war. There were 16 Union armies and 23 Confederate armies.
artillery	A term usually referring to some type of cannon. Field artillery were mobile, while heavy artillery were usually fixed as in defense of a fort..
assassinate	To murder a political official.
barbette	A raised wooden platform that allowed artillery to be fired over a wall.
barrel	The long metal tube on a gun the bullet is fired through.
battalion	A unit of soldiers. Two squadrons formed a battalion. Three battalions formed a regiment.
battery	The basic unit of soldiers in an artillery regiment. Comprised of 6 cannons, 155 men, 1 captain, 30 officers 2 buglers, 52 drivers, and 70 cannoneers.

battle	A military confrontation between two opposing forces.
bayonet	A metal blade attached to the end of a rifle and used as a spear.
bivouac	Hastily made shelters of plants or branches.
blockade	An effort to keep ships from entering or leaving ports.
border states	Maryland, Kentucky, Delaware and Missouri.
bounty	A sum of money paid to enlist in the military.
breech-loading	Rifles that were loaded in the middle, between the barrel and the stock, instead of from the end.
brevet	An honorary field promotion.
brigade	A unit of soldiers consisting of four or five regiments.
bummers	Soldiers who foraged for supplies.
caisson	A two-wheeled cart used to carry ammunition. A single cannon usually had two caissons, each with 150 projectiles.
caliber	The distance around the inside of a gun barrel measured in thousandths of an inch.
campaign	A series of military operations forming a particular phase of the war.
canister	A projectile fired from a cannon that is filled with 35 iron balls that scatter like pellets.
cap	a tiny brass shell that ignites the gunpowder in a percussion rifle or musket.
carbine	A breech-loading, single-shot rifle.
carpetbagger	A Northerner who gained political control in the South with the black vote.

cartridge	This was loaded into the rifle or musket to be fired. It included a bullet or projectile and wrapped paper containing gunpowder.
cascabel	The large round knob on a cannon.
casualty	A soldier who is wounded, killed, captured or missing in action.
cavalry	A branch of the military trained to fight on horses.
colors	A flag with the name and insignia of a specific military unit.
commissioned officer	An officer holding a certificate giving military rank.
commutation	$500 paid to avoid military service. 87,000 men avoided the draft this way.
company	A group of 50 to 100 soldiers led by a captain.
confederacy	Another name for the Confederate States of America or the South.
confederate	Someone loyal to the South during the war.
corps	A large group of soldiers led by a general. Usually made up of two or more divisions.
draft	A forced induction into military service.
earthwork	A trench or mound made of earth.
emancipation	Freedom from slavery.
enfilade	To fire along the length of the enemy line.
engagement	A battle.
enlist	To willingly join the military.
federal	Another name for the Union or Northern government.
foraging	To live off the land by stealing.

formation	Arrangement of troops for battle or marching.
fortification	Something that slows an enemy charge or makes a defensive position stronger.
furlough	A temporary leave.
garrison	A group of soldiers stationed at a military post.
goober pea	Southern term for peanut.
hardtack	A hard, and often worm-infested biscuit used as a source of food.
howitzer	A long-range piece of artillery.
infantry	Soldiers trained to fight on foot.
ironclad	A ship protected by armor, usually made of iron.
lunette	A two or three sided fort.
mason-Dixon line	A symbolic boundary between free and slave states. It was originally from a survey line around 1760.
militia	Troops, similar to the National Guard, who are only called on in an emergency.
minie ball	An elongated lead projectile designed by French Captain Claude-Etienne Minie.
mortar	A large artillery piece, with a short barrel, designed to throw heavy projectiles at high angles.
musket	A gun with a long, smooth barrel.
muster	To enlist a group of soldiers into military service.
muzzle-loading	A gun that is loaded from the end by putting the gunpowder and projectile down the barrel.

navy	The branch of the military that fought on ships, either on rivers or at sea.
north	Another name for the Union or the United States of America.
officer	A ranking soldier able to issue commands.
ordnance	A group of guns, ammunition, vehicles and equipment used in combat.
peculiar institution	Southern nickname for slavery.
percussion arm	A musket that requires a small cap to fire.
perish	To die or cease to exist.
picket	Soldiers posted on guard duty to warn the main force of attack.
pontoon	Connected, flat-bottomed wooden boats used to form a temporary bridge across rivers.
private	The lowest rank in the army.
rations	Food provided to the soldiers.
rebel	Someone loyal to the South during the war.
reconstruction	The period from 1865 to 1877, where the Southern states were rebuilt and brought back into the Union.
recruit	A person who enlists in the military.
regiment	A unit of the military made up of about 1,000 men.
revolver	A small gun, with a revolving chamber, holding about six bullets able to be fired rapidly without reloading.
rifle-musket	A gun with a long grooved barrel.

rout	A crushing defeat.
secession	The act of the Southern states withdrawing from the United States of America.
sentry	A soldier on guard duty.
shell	A hollow metal case containing an explosive charge.
siege	Blocking the supply lines and escape routes of a city to force it to surrender.
skirmish	A minor fight.
slavery	When African-Americans were owned and forced into labor.
small arms	A weapon carried and fired by hand, like a rifle or pistol.
smoothbore	A type of musket with a smooth barrel that fired round lead balls. They were not very accurate.
south	Another name for the Confederate States of America.
surrender	To give up and admit defeat.
sutler	Civilian merchants licensed to sell supplies and food to soldiers.
sympathizer	Someone who supports a cause.
tariff	Taxes placed on imported goods.
theater	An area where fighting takes place.
torpedo	Referred to today as mines, either floating in the path of a ship or buried in the ground.
total war	The act of destroying homes and crops of civilians in enemy territory.

union	Another name for the United States of America or the North.
veteran	A former member of the military.
volunteer	Someone who voluntarily enlists in the military.
west point	A famous military academy that many Civil War officers, in both the North and South, graduated.
Yankee	Someone loyal to the North.
zouave	A special unit of soldiers known for their colorful costumes and fierce fighting style.

References

Electronic References.

- 140th NYVI Living History Organization http://www.ggw.org/users/u140th/ Last Visited: February, 2007.
- 1938 Gettysburg Reunion http://encarta.msn.com/sidebar_461500346/1938_Gettysburg_Reunion.html Last Visited: February, 2007.
- 20th Maine http://20thmainevolunteers.com/ Last Visited: February, 2007.
- 20th Maine http://en.wikipedia.org/wiki/20th_Maine Last Visited: February, 2007.
- 4th & 5th Grade US History Sources - Civil War http://www.geocities.com/EnchantedForest/Tower/1217/civwar.html Last Visited: February, 2007.
- 54th Massachusetts http://en.wikipedia.org/wiki/54th_Massachusetts Last Visited: February, 2007.
- 69th New York http://www.69thnysv.org/ Last Visited: February, 2007.
- Abraham Lincoln and Jefferson Davis http://www.izzianne.com/notes/FALL2002/IAD125/Final/lincolndavis.html Last Visited: February, 2007.
- Aerial Photos of Gettysburg http://terraserver-usa.com/image.aspx?T=1&S=11&Z=18&X=774&Y=11023&W=2 Last Visited: February, 2007.
- African-Americans in the Civil War http://www.itd.nps.gov/cwss/history/aa_history.htm Last Visited: February, 2007.
- Amazon.com (Books and Movies) http://www.amazon.com Last Visited: February, 2007.
- American Civil War - Northern Leadership http://www.swcivilwar.com/cw_northern.html Last Visited: February, 2007.

- American Civil War - Southern Leadership http://www.swcivilwar.com/cw_southern.html Last Visited: February, 2007.
- American Civil War – Wikipedia http://en.wikipedia.org/wiki/American_Civil_War Last Visited: February, 2007.
- American Civil War http://www.bmarch.atfreeweb.com/civil_war.htm Last Visited: February, 2007.
- American Civil War Association http://acwa.org/ Last Visited: February, 2007.
- American Civil War Glossary http://www.civilwar.org/historyclassroom/hc_glossary.htm Last Visited: February, 2007.
- American Civil War Home Page http://www.civilwarhome.com/ Last Visited: February, 2007.
- American Civil War Homepage http://sunsite.utk.edu/civil-war/ Last Visited: February, 2007.
- American Civil War Quotes - General Ulysses S. Grant http://www.brotherswar.com/Civil_War_Quotes_4a.htm Last Visited: February, 2007.
- American Civil War Reenactor Images http://www.wildwestweb.net/cw.html Last Visited: February, 2007.
- Army of the Tennessee http://en.wikipedia.org/wiki/Army_of_the_Tennessee Last Visited: February, 2007.
- Battle of Gettysburg http://en.wikipedia.org/wiki/Battle_of_Gettysburg Last Visited: February, 2007.
- Bbunny's Historical Hubbub http://members.tripod.com/BooneBunny/morehubbub.html Last Visited: February, 2007.
- Berdans Sharpshooters http://www.berdansharpshooters.com/berdanbio.html Last Visited: February, 2007.

- Brevet Union Generals of the Civil War http://www.alia.org.au/~kwebb/Brevets/ Last Visited: February, 2007.
- Buffalo Soldiers http://en.wikipedia.org/wiki/Buffalo_Soldiers Last Visited: February, 2007.
- Cashtown Inn http://www.cashtowninn.com/ Last Visited: February, 2007.
- Casualties of the Civil War http://www.civilwarhome.com/casualties.htm Last Visited: February, 2007.
- Children in the Civil War http://www.brunswick.k12.me.us/lon/civilwar/children/essays.html Last Visited: February, 2007.
- Civil War - 1861-1865 http://homework.syosset.k12.ny.us/teachers/pfitzger/civil_war.htm Last Visited: February, 2007.
- Civil War - 8th Grade Resources http://www.knoxville.k12.ia.us/ms/library/civil_war8.htm Last Visited: February, 2007.
- Civil War – Resources http://members.aol.com/TeacherNet/civilwar.html Last Visited: February, 2007.
- Civil War – Web http://www.sonofthesouth.net/ Last Visited: February, 2007.
- Civil War Alphabetic List of American Civil War Battles http://americancivilwar.com/statepic/alpha.html Last Visited: February, 2007.
- Civil War Archive Home Page http://www.civilwararchive.com/ Last Visited: February, 2007.
- Civil War Artillery Page http://www.cwartillery.org/artillery.html Last Visited: February, 2007.
- Civil War at a Glance http://www.pueblo.gsa.gov/cic_text/misc/civilwar/civilwar.htm Last Visited: February, 2007.

- Civil War Battle Names http://www.civilwarhome.com/battlenames.htm Last Visited: February, 2007.
- Civil War Battle Names http://www.civilwarhome.com/battlenames.htm Last Visited: February, 2007.
- Civil War Battlefields http://www.cwbattlefields.com/index.html Last Visited: February, 2007.
- Civil War Battles http://americanhistory.about.com/od/civilwarbattles/ Last Visited: February, 2007.
- Civil War Battles http://www.homepages.dsu.edu/jankej/civilwar/battles.htm Last Visited: February, 2007.
- Civil War Battles http://www.sonofthesouth.net/leefoundation/civil-war-battles.htm Last Visited: February, 2007.
- Civil War Battles http://www2.lhric.org/pocantico/civilwar/battles.htm Last Visited: February, 2007.
- Civil War Battles by State http://www.cr.nps.gov/hps/abpp/battles/bystate.htm Last Visited: February, 2007.
- Civil War Bullets http://www.cwbullet.org/bullet-resources.php Last Visited: February, 2007.
- Civil War Cadets Roundtable http://www.dentistry.com/cwrt/reenactor.html Last Visited: February, 2007.
- Civil War Children http://www2.lhric.org/pocantico/civilwar/children.htm Last Visited: February, 2007.
- Civil War Encyclopedia http://blueandgraytrail.com/cwe Last Visited: February, 2007.
- Civil War Era Women Physicians http://galenpress.com/extras/extra30.htm Last Visited: February, 2007.

- Civil War Facts http://www.civil-war.ws/facts/ Last Visited: February, 2007.
- Civil War Flags http://www.civil-war.ws/flags/ Last Visited: February, 2007.
- Civil War Flags http://www.fortunecity.com/victorian/museum/63/flags/main.html# Last Visited: February, 2007.
- Civil War for Fifth Graders http://www.radford.edu/~sbisset/civilwar.htm Last Visited: February, 2007.
- Civil War for Kids http://www2.lhric.org/pocantico/civilwar/cwar.htm Last Visited: February, 2007.
- Civil War Generals http://www.sonofthesouth.net/prod012.htm Last Visited: February, 2007.
- Civil War Generals http://www.teacheroz.com/Civil_War_Battles.htm#generals Last Visited: February, 2007.
- Civil War Ghost Stories http://www.bookguy.com/civilwar/ghosts.htm Last Visited: February, 2007.
- Civil War Ghosts http://www.ghostresearch.org/articles/battle.html Last Visited: February, 2007.
- Civil War Ghosts http://www.ghostvillage.com/legends/2006/legends44_09152006.shtml Last Visited: February, 2007.
- Civil War Ghosts http://www.shadowseekers.org/civilwarghosts.html Last Visited: February, 2007.
- Civil War Glossary http://www.civilwarweapons.net/html/glossary.html Last Visited: February, 2007.
- Civil War History Central http://www.multied.com/CivilWar/ Last Visited: February, 2007.

- Civil War Home Page http://www.civil-war.net/ Last Visited: February, 2007.
- Civil War Hospitals http://www.geocities.com/civilwarfieldhospital/ Last Visited: February, 2007.
- Civil War Hospitals, Surgeons, and Nurses http://www.civilwarhome.com/hospitalssurgeonsnurses.htm Last Visited: February, 2007.
- Civil War Image Map http://homepage.floodcity.net/users/mastdog/states.html Last Visited: February, 2007.
- Civil War in Miniature http://www.civilwarmini.com/ Last Visited: February, 2007.
- Civil War Interactive http://www.civilwarinteractive.com/ Last Visited: February, 2007.
- Civil War Links http://www.suite101.com/links.cfm/civil_war Last Visited: February, 2007.
- Civil War Links http://www.teacheroz.com/civilwar.htm Last Visited: February, 2007.
- Civil War Links-Reenacting http://www.civil-war.net/searchlinks.asp?searchlinks=Reenacting Last Visited: February, 2007.
- Civil War Map of State Battle Locations http://americancivilwar.com/statepic/ Last Visited: February, 2007.
- Civil War Mascot http://www.civilwar.vt.edu/featured/littlemascot.html Last Visited: February, 2007.
- Civil War Mascots http://oha.ci.alexandria.va.us/fortward/special-sections/mascots/ Last Visited: February, 2007.
- Civil War Mascots http://www.floridareenactorsonline.com/mascots.htm Last Visited: February, 2007.

- Civil War Medicine http://homepages.dsu.edu/jankej/civilwar/medicine.htm Last Visited: February, 2007.
- Civil War MIDI Page http://midistudio.com/Legal/civilwarES.html Last Visited: February, 2007.
- Civil War Money http://www.coinfacts.com Last Visited: February, 2007.
- Civil War Music http://home.att.net/~dmercado/music.htm Last Visited: February, 2007.
- Civil War Music http://www.pbs.org/civilwar/classroom/lesson_music.html Last Visited: February, 2007.
- Civil War Music http://www.us-civilwar.com/music.htm Last Visited: February, 2007.
- Civil War Music Site Songs http://www.civilwarmusic.net/songs.php Last Visited: February, 2007.
- Civil War Photographs http://712educators.about.com/od/historycw/a/cwphmenu.htm Last Visited: February, 2007.
- Civil War Photos.Net – Civilians http://www.civilwarphotos.net/files/civilians.htm Last Visited: February, 2007.
- Civil War Pictures Database http://www.civilwar-pictures.com/ Last Visited: February, 2007.
- Civil War Preservation Trust http://en.wikipedia.org/wiki/Civil_War_Preservation_Trust Last Visited: February, 2007.
- Civil War Prison Elmira http://home.jam.rr.com/rjcourt52/cwprisons/elmiran.htm Last Visited: February, 2007.
- Civil War Prisons http://homepages.dsu.edu/jankej/civilwar/prisons.htm Last Visited: February, 2007.

- Civil War Ranks http://www.civilwarhome.com/cwrank.htm Last Visited: February, 2007.
- Civil War Ranks http://www.friesian.com/rank.htm Last Visited: February, 2007.
- Civil War Reenacting http://en.wikipedia.org/wiki/American_Civil_War_reenactment Last Visited: February, 2007.
- Civil War Reenacting http://mtsu32.mtsu.edu:11263/Civil%20War%20Reenactor.htm Last Visited: February, 2007.
- Civil War Reenacting http://nps-vip.net/history/reenact/ Last Visited: February, 2007.
- Civil War Reenacting http://sunsite.utk.edu/civil-war/warweb.html#reenactors Last Visited: February, 2007.
- Civil War Reenacting http://www.texasrifles.org/reenact.htm Last Visited: February, 2007.
- Civil War Reenactment Headquarters http://www.sutler.net/howtoguide.asp Last Visited: February, 2007.
- Civil War Reunion http://home.att.net/~DogSgt/reunion_3_part1.html Last Visited: February, 2007.
- Civil War Rosters by State http://www.geocities.com/Area51/Lair/3680/cw/cw.html Last Visited: February, 2007.
- Civil War Sites http://usa-civil-war.com/Civil_War/cw_sites.html Last Visited: February, 2007.
- Civil War Soldiers and Units http://www.cwc.lsu.edu/links/cwsuinfo.htm Last Visited: February, 2007.
- Civil War Terminology http://civilwarmini.com/terms.htm Last Visited: February, 2007.

- Civil War Timeline http://www.pinzler.com/ushistory/cwtimeline.html Last Visited: February, 2007.
- Civil War Unit Study http://home.rochester.rr.com/inwoods/civilwar.htm Last Visited: February, 2007.
- Civil War Weapons - Shoulder Arms http://www.civilwarweapons.net/ Last Visited: February, 2007.
- Civil War Weapons http://www.civilwarhome.com/civilwarweapons.htm Last Visited: February, 2007.
- Civil War Weapons http://www.geocities.com/Athens/3644/Weapons.html Last Visited: February, 2007.
- Civil War Weapons http://www.weaponsofolde.com/ciwarwe.html Last Visited: February, 2007.
- Civil War Weapons and Technology http://www.teacheroz.com/Civil_War_Weapons.htm Last Visited: February, 2007.
- Civil War Websites http://members.aol.com/veterans/warlib6l.htm Last Visited: February, 2007.
- Civil War Websites http://www.bcpl.net/~perhllms/socstud/civwar/ Last Visited: February, 2007.
- Civil War Women http://mariah.stonemarche.org/livhis/women/ Last Visited: February, 2007.
- Civil War Women http://www.libraryautomation.com/nymas/civilwarwomen.html Last Visited: February, 2007.
- Civil War Women http://www.wmol.com/whalive/cww.htm Last Visited: February, 2007.

- Civil War Zouave Units http://members.tripod.com/%7EShaung/cwuni.html Last Visited: February, 2007.
- Civil War, in U.S. History - Yahoo! Education http://education.yahoo.com/reference/encyclopedia/entry/CivilWarUS Last Visited: February, 2007.
- Civil War.com http://www.civilwar.com/ Last Visited: February, 2007.
- Civil Wars of the World http://en.wikipedia.org/wiki/List_of_civil_wars Last Visited: February, 2007.
- Civilwarsite.com – Songs http://www.civilwarsite.com/songs.html Last Visited: February, 2007.
- Confederate Currency http://www.csacurrency.com/ Last Visited: February, 2007.
- Confederate Dollar http://en.wikipedia.org/wiki/Confederate_States_of_America_dollar Last Visited: February, 2007.
- Confederate Flags of the American Civil War http://americancivilwar.com/south/conflag/southflg.html Last Visited: February, 2007.
- Confederate group says Gettysburg art show desecrates flag http://www.knoxstudio.com/shns/story.cfm?pk=CONFEDERATE-09-02-04&cat=AN Last Visited: March, 2007.
- Confederate Naval Arms http://www.navyarms.com/html/cw-confed.html Last Visited: February, 2007.
- Confederate Regimental History Links http://www.tarleton.edu/~kjones/confeds.html Last Visited: February, 2007.
- Congressional Medal of Honor http://en.wikipedia.org/wiki/Medal_of_Honor Last Visited: February, 2007.
- Corcoran http://www.multied.com/Bio/UGENS/USACorcoran.html Last Visited: February, 2007.

- Dukes of Hazzard nixed in Cincinnati http://news.yahoo.com/s/ap/20070319/ap_en_tv/dukes_of_hazzard_orchestra Last Visited: March, 2007.
- Duryee's Zouaves http://www.webcom.com/kepi/ Last Visited: February, 2007.
- Educational Weblinks http://www.civilwar.org/historyclassroom/hc_weblinks.htm Last Visited: February, 2007.
- Elmira Prison Camp http://www.angelfire.com/ny5/elmiraprison/index.html Last Visited: February, 2007.
- Endangered Battlefields – Maryland http://www.civilwar.org/landpreservation/l_en_Maryland.htm Last Visited: February, 2007.
- Endangered Battlefields http://www.civilwarnews.com/archive/articles/endangered_battlefields.htm Last Visited: February, 2007.
- Famous Civil War Generals http://ourworld.compuserve.com/homepages/allender/famcwgen.htm Last Visited: February, 2007.
- Famous Civil War Units http://civilwar.bluegrass.net/FamousUnits/index.html Last Visited: February, 2007.
- Famous Horses of the Civil War http://www.civilwarhome.com/horses.htm Last Visited: February, 2007.
- Fort Ward Museum-Animal Mascots of the Civil War http://oha.alexandriava.gov/fortward/special-sections/mascots/ Last Visited: February, 2007.
- Fredericksburg and Spotsylvania http://www.eriksmith.com/VADC/fredericksburgNBp2.htm Last Visited: February, 2007.
- Fredericksburg.com - Civil War Glossary http://www.fredericksburg.com/CivilWar/Re-enact/Teaching/Teaching/Education/glossary Last Visited: February, 2007.

- Generals and Other Noteworthy People From the Civil War http://www.aboutfamouspeople.com/article1142.html Last Visited: February, 2007.
- Generals of the American Civil War http://www.generalsandbrevets.com/ Last Visited: February, 2007.
- Generals of the Civil War http://homepages.dsu.edu/jankej/civilwar/generals.htm Last Visited: February, 2007.
- Geographic Information Systems for Battlefield Preservation http://www.civilwar.gatech.edu/ Last Visited: February, 2007.
- Gett Kidz - Civil War Music http://www.nps.gov/gett/gettkidz/music.htm Last Visited: February, 2007.
- Gettysburg - The Final Reunion http://www.gettysburg.com/livinghistory/pastpics/1938/193801.htm Last Visited: February, 2007.
- Gettysburg Address http://www.gettysburgaddress.com/HTMLS/v.tour.html Last Visited: February, 2007.
- Gettysburg College's Hate Crime 'Artist' http://www.lewrockwell.com/dilorenzo/dilorenzo76.html Last Visited: March, 2007.
- Gettysburg Ghosts http://www.2bridges.com/gettysghosts.htm Last Visited: February, 2007.
- Gettysburg Ghosts http://www.gettysburgghosts.net/ Last Visited: February, 2007.
- Gettysburg Ghosts http://www.gotogettysburg.com/hauntedgettysburgghosts.htm Last Visited: February, 2007.
- Gettysburg Ghosts-Kids Pages http://www.gettysburgghosts.net/kidspages.htm Last Visited: February, 2007.
- Gettysburg Links http://www.virtualgettysburg.com/connect/links/ Last Visited: February, 2007.

- Gettysburg National Military Park Kidzpage http://www.nps.gov/gett/gettkidz/kidzindex.htm Last Visited: February, 2007.
- Gettysburg.com http://www.gettysburg.com/ Last Visited: February, 2007.
- Ghosts of Gettysburg http://www.ghostsofgettysburg.com/ Last Visited: February, 2007.
- Glossary - Civil War Battalions http://members.aol.com/DAp4477575/page15.htm Last Visited: February, 2007.
- Grand Army of the Republic http://en.wikipedia.org/wiki/GAR Last Visited: February, 2007.
- Great Reunion http://www.members.tripod.com/beag27/reunion.html Last Visited: February, 2007.
- Harriet Jacobs - Linda Brent http://www.wsu.edu/~campbelld/amlit/jacobs.htm Last Visited: February, 2007.
- Harriet Tubman Conductor of the Underground Railroad http://americancivilwar.com/women/harriet_tubman.html Last Visited: February, 2007.
- Haunted Gettysburg http://www.hauntedgettysburg.com/ Last Visited: February, 2007.
- Haunted PA http://www.hauntedpa.com/textSite/gt10.shtml Last Visited: February, 2007.
- Haunted Virginia http://www.hauntedtraveler.com/haunted_virginia.htm Last Visited: February, 2007.
- Hiram Berdan http://en.wikipedia.org/wiki/Hiram_Berdan Last Visited: February, 2007.
- History of the Civil War http://www.vgsd.org/~kgallagher/ Last Visited: February, 2007.

- History Place - U.S. Civil War 1861-1865 http://www.historyplace.com/civilwar/index.html Last Visited: February, 2007.
- Horses of the Civil War Leaders http://www.civilwarhome.com/warhorses.htm Last Visited: February, 2007.
- Images of the American Civil War http://www.civil-war.net/cw_images/files/infantry.htm Last Visited: February, 2007.
- Images of the Civil War - Confederate Army Officers http://www.treasurenet.com/images/civilwar/civil021.shtml Last Visited: February, 2007.
- Indiana in the Civil War http://www.indianainthecivilwar.com/ Last Visited: February, 2007.
- Irish Brigade http://en.wikipedia.org/wiki/Irish_Brigade_%28US%29 Last Visited: February, 2007.
- Irish Brigade History http://irishvolunteers.tripod.com/irish_brigade_history.htm Last Visited: February, 2007.
- Ironclads and Blockade Runners http://www.wideopenwest.com/~jenkins/ironclads/ironclad.htm Last Visited: February, 2007.
- James A. Hard http://www.vintageviews.org/vv-tl/Photos/pages/hard.html Last Visited: February, 2007.
- Jefferson Davis President Confederate States of America http://americancivilwar.com/south/jeffdavi.html Last Visited: February, 2007.
- Jennie Wade House http://www.jennie-wade-house.com/ Last Visited: February, 2007.
- Julia Dent Grant, 1826-1902 http://www.pbs.org/wgbh/amex/grant/peopleevents/p_jgrant.html Last Visited: February, 2007.
- Just Curious - Civil War http://www.suffolk.lib.ny.us/youth/jccivil.html Last Visited: February, 2007.

- Kansas in the Civil War http://skyways.lib.ks.us/kansas/genweb/civilwar/index.html Last Visited: February, 2007.
- Kentucky Civil War Preservation Program http://www.state.ky.us/agencies/khc/civilwar.htm Last Visited: February, 2007.
- Leaders and Battles Database http://www.lbdb.com/TMDisplayBattle.cfm?BID=127&WID=2 Last Visited: February, 2007.
- Lincoln and the Civil War http://lincolnandthecivilwar.com/ Last Visited: February, 2007.
- Mary Boykin Chesnutt http://docsouth.unc.edu/southlit/chesnut/bio.html Last Visited: February, 2007.
- Maryland Women's Hall of Fame - Anna Ella Carroll http://www.mdarchives.state.md.us/msa/educ/exhibits/womenshall/html/carroll.htmlLast Visited: February, 2007.
- Military Ghosts http://www.militaryghosts.com/ Last Visited: February, 2007.
- Mindy's Civil War Page http://members.aol.com/mindysmazes/civilwar/glossary.htm Last Visited: February, 2007.
- Minorities in the War http://militaryhistory.about.com/cs/minorities/ Last Visited: February, 2007.
- Modern Photos of Civil War Sites http://www.civilwaralbum.com/index.html Last Visited: February, 2007.
- Monocacy National Battlefield - Flags http://www.nps.gov/archive/mono/mo_flags.htm Last Visited: February, 2007.
- More Civil War Slang http://www.members.tripod.com/BooneBunny/slang.html Last Visited: February, 2007.
- Mr. Lincoln and Freedom http://www.mrlincolnandfreedom.org/inside.asp?ID=54&subjectID=3 Last Visited: February, 2007.

- Mrnussbaum.com - Civil War http://www.mrnussbaum.com/civilwargenerals.htm Last Visited: February, 2007.
- Music of the American Civil War http://www.pdmusic.org/civilwar.html Last Visited: February, 2007.
- Naming the American Civil War http://en.wikipedia.org/wiki/Naming_the_American_Civil_War Last Visited: February, 2007.
- NARA - Research - Civil War http://www.archives.gov/research/civil-war/ Last Visited: February, 2007.
- National Civil War Association http://www.ncwa.org/ Last Visited: February, 2007.
- National Civil War Museum http://www.nationalcivilwarmuseum.org/ Last Visited: February, 2007.
- New Yorkers Active in the Underground Railroad http://www.nyhistory.com/ugrr/people.htm Last Visited: February, 2007.
- No Casino in Gettysburg http://www.nocasinogettysburg.com/index.html Last Visited: February, 2007.
- North-South Alliance http://www.nsalliance.org/ Last Visited: February, 2007.
- Official Record of the War of the Rebellion http://www.civilwarhome.com/records.htm Last Visited: February, 2007.
- Ohio in the Civil War http://www.ohiocivilwar.com/cw23.html Last Visited: February, 2007.
- Old Abe - The War Eagle http://museum.dva.state.wi.us/News_Releases/oldabe0404.asp Last Visited: February, 2007.
- Old Abe http://home.centurytel.net/dgeist/oldabeinfo.htm Last Visited: February, 2007.

- Preserving Historic Fredericksburg http://www.fredericksburg.com/CivilWar/Preservation Last Visited: February, 2007.
- Rebel flag 'interpreted' http://www.washtimes.com/national/20040829-114525-7001r.htm Last Visited: March, 2007.
- Reenacting and Preservation http://homepage.mac.com/fjordaniv/cwreenactors/preservation.html Last Visited: February, 2007.
- Respectful Insolence http://scienceblogs.com/insolence/2006/10/persistence_of_controversy_over_the_conf_1.php Last Visited: March, 2007.
- Selected Civil War Photographs Home Page http://memory.loc.gov/ammem/cwphtml/cwphome.html Last Visited: February, 2007.
- Slavery http://www.civilwarhome.com/slavery.htm Last Visited: February, 2007.
- Slavery in America http://www.socialstudiesforkids.com/subjects/slavery.htm Last Visited: February, 2007.
- Sons of Union Veterans of the Civil War http://suvcw.org/past/wfvlewis.htm Last Visited: February, 2007.
- Stephen Foster Songs - Battle Cry of Freedom http://www.stephen-foster-songs.de/Amsong06.htm Last Visited: February, 2007.
- Timeline of the Civil War http://memory.loc.gov/ammem/cwphtml/tl1861.html Last Visited: February, 2007.
- Treasurenet Historical Image Collection http://www.treasurenet.com/images/ Last Visited: February, 2007.
- U.S. Civil War - Info Links http://www.socialstudiesforkids.com/subjects/civilwar.htm Last Visited: February, 2007.
- U.S. Civil War Weapons http://realarmorofgod.com/civil-war-weapons.html Last Visited: February, 2007.

- U.S. Civil War Weapons http://www.nps.gov/gett/soldierlife/webguns.htm Last Visited: February, 2007.
- U.S. History - Civil War http://www.besthistorysites.net/USHistory_CivilWar.shtml Last Visited: February, 2007.
- Ulysses S. Grant and Robert E. Lee http://www.izzianne.com/notes/FALL2002/IAD125/Final/grantlee.html Last Visited: February, 2007.
- Uniforms of the Civil War http://www.kidport.com/RefLib/UsaHistory/CivilWar/Uniforms.htm#Union%20Uniforms Last Visited: February, 2007.
- Union Army Regimental History Links http://www.tarleton.edu/~kjones/unions.html Last Visited: February, 2007.
- Union Regiments - New York http://www.civilwararchive.com/unionny.htm Last Visited: February, 2007.
- United Confederate Veterans http://en.wikipedia.org/wiki/United_Confederate_Veterans Last Visited: February, 2007.
- United Daughters of the Confederacy http://en.wikipedia.org/wiki/United_Daughters_of_the_Confederacy Last Visited: February, 2007.
- University of Rochester and the Civil War http://www.lib.rochester.edu/index.cfm?PAGE=1796 Last Visited: February, 2007.
- US Civil War Generals http://sunsite.utk.edu/civil-war/generals.html Last Visited: February, 2007.
- USN Ships - USS Monitor http://www.history.navy.mil/photos/sh-usn/usnsh-m/monitor.htm Last Visited: February, 2007.
- Varina Howell Davis http://www.us-civilwar.com/varina.htm Last Visited: February, 2007.
- Warren Carman-Medal of Honor http://www.homeofheroes.com/moh/citations_1862_cwa/carman_warren.html Last Visited: February, 2007.

- Wars of the World http://www.globalsecurity.org/military/world/war/index.html Last Visited: February, 2007.
- Washington Monument State Park http://www.dnr.state.md.us/publiclands/western/washington.html Last Visited: February, 2007.
- Weapons of the Civil War http://members.tripod.com/~ProlificPains/wpns.htm Last Visited: February, 2007.
- William Clarke Quantrill, Spies, Raiders and Partisans http://www.wtv-zone.com/civilwar/wquantrill.html Last Visited: February, 2007.
- Women in the Civil War http://userpages.aug.com/captbarb/femvets2.html Last Visited: February, 2007.
- Women of the American Civil War Era Last Visited: February, 2007.
- Women Spies - Mary Elizabeth Bowser http://www.sameshield.com/spies/bowser.html Last Visited: February, 2007.
- Women Spies http://womenshistory.about.com/library/misc/cw/bl_cw_spies_union.htm Last Visited: February, 2007.

Printed Materials.

- Cohen, Stan. Hands Across the Wall - The 50th and 75th Reunions of the Gettysburg Battle. Charleston, West Virginia: Pictoral Histories Publishing Company, Inc., 1982.
- Davis, Burke. The Civil War: Strange and Fascinating Facts. New York: Wings Books, 1960.
- Davis, William C. Civil War: A Complete Photographic History. New York: Tess Press, 2000.
- Garrison, Webb. Civil War Curiosities. Nashville: Rutledge Hill Press, 1994.
- Earp, Charles Albert. The 75th Reunion at Gettysburg - My Interviews with the Veterans. Linthicum, Maryland: Toomey Press, 2003.
- Frassanito, William A. Gettysburg - Then and Now. Gettysburg, Pennsylvania: Thomas Publications, 1996.
- Nesbitt, Mark. Ghosts of Gettysburg. Gettysburg, Pennsylvania: Thomas Publications, 1995.
- Schildt, John W. Antietam Hospitals. Chewsville, Maryland: Antietam Publications, 1996.
- Schroeder, Patrick A. More Myths About Lee's Surrender. Lynchburg, Virginia: Schroeder Publications, 2004.
- Schroeder, Patrick A. Thirty Myths About Lee's Surrender. Lynchburg, Virginia: Schroeder Publications, 2004.
- Williams, Edward F. Great American Civil War Trivia. Nashville: Premium Press America, 1998.

About the Author

Richard Stephen Hartmetz was born in Rochester, NY on February 9, 1965. Richard has degrees in Computer Science, Special Education and Psychology.

He spent many years as a teacher in the Rochester City School District, East Irondequoit, St. Margaret Mary School and the School of the Holy Childhood where he was known as "Mr. H." He is now the CEO of Starry Night Publishing.com.

Richard is also the author of the "Murry Peterson" espionage series: "Spy Game," "Checkmate," "Deceit," "Failsafe," "Iron Curtain," "Echelon," and "The Final Countdown." He has also written "The Adventures of Robin Caruso," and the #1 bestseller "Secrets to Writing Well."

His other children's books "Marvin!, Marvin!, Marvin!," "Hurray For Marvin," "Super-Marvin," and "Marvin and Ted," which are currently available from Amazon.com, Barnes & Noble.com, Starry Night Publishing.com and many other fine booksellers.

Richard wrote his first story, entitled “The Dog Catcher is Coming,” when he was only six years old and has been writing since, also teaching several writing workshops.

You may connect with Richard, Murry Peterson, Robin Caruso and Starry Night Publishing on Facebook and at

www.starrynightpublishing.com.

"I was pinned between the two most dangerous things on the island! I was either going to be murdered by the pirates, or eaten alive by the tiger, and right now, I wasn't liking either of those options."

Robin Caruso is a typical teenage girl, who wants to live anything but the typical life. She longs for adventure and attempts to persuade her parents to allow her to become the youngest person ever to sail around the world solo. At first, they refuse, but after their daughter is branded a hero during a dramatic at-sea rescue, they have little choice but to consent.

Months later, the preparations are made, but a last minute injunction is filed to prevent the voyage from taking place and Robin must stage a daring escape before she is able to get underway. Chased by the authorities, at the mercy of nature, modern-day pirates, angry natives and her own doubts, this is truly the journey of a lifetime.

Join us for an adventure on the high seas with Robin while she risks life and limb to circumnavigate the globe in her one-person sailboat, learning that true courage comes from within and that living is the greatest adventure of all.

The Adventures of Robin Caruso

Gettysburg, Pennsylvania, the site of one of the greatest battles in history; now home to a sinister conspiracy dating back to the founding of the United States itself and reaching into the deepest and most secretive levels of the government; a conspiracy that threatens to plunge the world into a chasm of domination and nuclear devastation.

Muriel Peterson's grandfather is killed in 1976. Four years later, the guidance counselor at her new junior high school asks if she is a good American and offers to free her from the boredom of being a preteen in her small Pennsylvania town. He asks her to spy on a family of Russian immigrants suspected of stealing secrets for the KGB. She reluctantly accepts and begins to infiltrate the life of that fellow student and his family.

Murry slowly uncovers a conspiracy by a rogue Soviet general and someone inside the CIA to place sleeper agents throughout the country in an effort to start a war with the Soviet Union and replace the US government. Along the way, she discovers dark secrets long hidden by her handler, a mysterious FBI agent and even her deceased grandfather leading to a much larger conspiracy that threatens to pull a dark veil across the face of the entire world. All this while she attempts to deal with the pressures of growing up in a dysfunctional family, social isolation and young love.

Murry Peterson: Spy Game

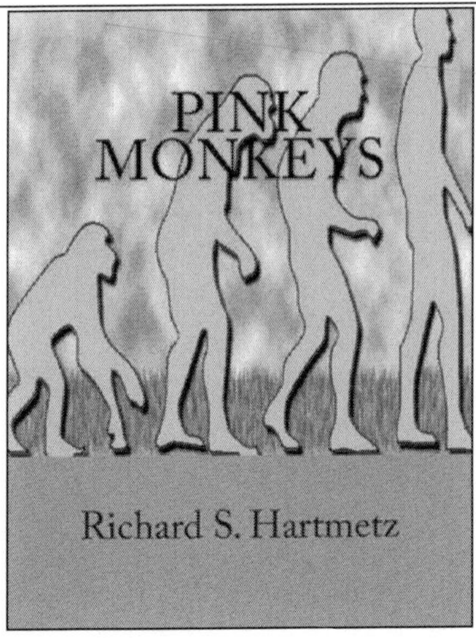

A little bird sits high on a wire, watching the strange pink monkeys below him. Father bird warns him that they are dangerous, but he is curious and decides to ask the other animals about them. He questions a robin, a horse, a cow, a honeybee, an ant, a dog, a deer, a rabbit, and an owl, all of whom warn him of the dangers connected to the fearsome beasts.

The owl tells the little bird how they fight in great wars, and participate in animal slavery, poisoning the air and water, and even killing their own kind. The little bird can scarcely believe that such creatures exist, so he goes out into the world to see for himself. Then he is injured by a giant metal beast and captured by one of the pink monkeys. Are they truly as fierce as he has been told, or will he need their help to survive?

This is a truly enlightening picture book sprinkled with healthy doses of introspection for everyone who has ever wondered what "animals" really think.

<u>Pink Monkeys</u>

Starry Night Classics:

Classic Stories from the Original Authors

Agatha Christie:
The Mysterious Affair At Styles
The Secret Adversary

Anna Sewell:
Black Beauty

Arthur Conan Doyle:
Sherlock Holmes - A Study In Scarlet
The Lost World

Charles Dickens:
A Christmas Carol
Great Expectations

Daniel Defoe:
Robinson Crusoe

Edgar Rice Burroughs:
The Land That Time Forgot
The People That Time Forgot
Out of Time's Abyss
A Princess of Mars
Tarzan of the Apes
At the Earth's Core

Emily Bronte:
Wuthering Heights

Frances Hodgson Burnett:
Little Lord Fauntleroy
The Secret Garden
A Little Princess

H. G. Wells:
The Time Machine
The Island of Doctor Moreau
The War of the Worlds
The Invisible Man

Howard R. Garis:
Uncle Wiggily Hops Along
Uncle Wiggily Seeks His Fortune
Uncle Wiggily Starts Off
Uncle Wiggily Travels On
Uncle Wiggily's Excursion
Uncle Wiggily's Expedition
Uncle Wiggily's Journey

Hugh Lofting:
The Story of Doctor Dolittle
The Voyages of Doctor Dolittle

J. M. Barrie:
Peter Pan

Jack London:
The Call of the Wild
White Fang
The Sea-Wolf

James Fenimore Cooper
The Last of the Mohicans

Jane Austen:
Sense and Sensibility
Pride and Prejudice
Persuasion

Johann David Wyss:
Swiss Family Robinson

Jules Verne:
Around the World in Eighty Days
Journey to the Center of the Earth
Twenty Thousand Leagues Under the Sea

L. Frank Baum:
The Wonderful Wizard of Oz

Lewis Carroll:
Alice in Wonderland
Through the Looking Glass

Louisa May Alcott:
Little Women
Little Men
Jo's Boys

Lucy Maud Montgomery:
Anne of Green Gables

Mark Twain:
Huckleberry Finn
Tom Sawyer
The Prince and the Pauper

Nathaniel Hawthorne:
The Scarlet Letter
The House of the Seven Gables
Twice Told Tales

Robert Louis Stevenson:
Treasure Island
Kidnapped
Dr. Jekyll and Mr. Hyde

Rudyard Kipling:
The Jungle Book
The Second Jungle Book

Stephen Crane:
The Red Badge of Courage

The Brothers Grimm:
Grimm's Fairy Tales

Edgar Allan Poe:
The Best of Poe

Mary Mapes Dodge:
Hans Brinker, or The Silver Skates

Kenneth Grahame:
The Wind in the Willows

L. Leslie Brooke:
The Story of the Three Little Pigs

Beatrix Potter:
The Tale of Peter Rabbit

Charlotte Bronte:
Jane Eyre

Howard Pyle:
Robin Hood

The American Civil War

Starry Night Biographies:

The Stories of the People Who Left Their Mark on the World

The Life of Mary Jemison
by James E. Seaver

The Autobiography of Benjamin Franklin
by Benjamin Franklin

Richard S. Hartmetz

Starry Night History:

The Stories of Our Lives

Presidential Inaugural Addresses (1789-2009)
by Richard S. Hartmetz

The History of American Aviation and Space Travel
by Richard S. Hartmetz

The American Civil War
by Richard S. Hartmetz

Starry Night Books:

Your Stories

What Did I Do Wrong?
by Eveline Sandy

Teeta Heads West
by Bonnie West

The Dhikr of Authenticity
by Dawud Abdur-Rahman

Theft of a Nation
Treason
The CONstitution That Never Was
by Ralph Boryszewski

Wonderings: Poems of Peace and Solace
by Rosemarie MacCheyene

My Dog Fluffy
by Andrew Stedmann

Pink Monkeys
The Adventures of Robin Caruso
Secrets to Writing Well
Marvin and Ted
Marvin! Marvin! Marvin!
Hurray For Marvin
Super-Marvin
by Richard S. Hartmetz

Murry Peterson Books:
Spy Game
Checkmate
Deceit
Failsafe
Iron Curtain
Echelon
The Final Countdown

THE FUTURE IS NOW!

Gone are the days when an author would sit in front of an old manual typewriter, rubbing holes in the paper or filling their office garbage cans with unsalvageable scrap. The publishing industry is evolving. The old publishing houses are becoming dinosaurs. E-books are everywhere. They are cheaper than old-fashioned books, use less paper and ink, faster to produce, take up less space and can be read on any computer, e-reader or Smartphone.

Success comes to those who make opportunities happen, not those who wait for opportunities to happen. You can be successful too, you just have to try...

A recent poll suggested that nearly 85% of parents would encourage their child to read a book on an e-reader. More than 1 in 5 of us owns an e-reading device and the number is climbing rapidly. For every 100 hardcover books that Amazon sells, it sells 143 e-books. They also never go out of print!

Hundreds of thousands of independent authors, just like you, are selling their profitable work as you read this. E-book sales have grown over 200% in the past year and account for more than $1 billion in annual sales.

Chances are, you don't even know the difference between a PDF, mobi, ePub, doc, azw, or the fifteen other competing formats struggling to coexist on the sixteen types of e-reader devices such as the Kindle or the Nook. Even if you are able to keep up with all the devices and their formats, do you want to spend the money for expensive software to convert your files, or the many hours it will take to figure out how it works? Will you be able to create an interactive table of contents?

Our editors are professionals with experience in computer science, graphic design and publishing. We can do the work or you, creating a top-notch book that you will be proud of. Of course, you still have to write it, but that's the fun part...